HOW DO I LOVE ME ?

2nd Edition

HOW DO I LOVE ME?

HELEN M. JOHNSON · 2nd Edition

Sheffield Publishing Company

Salem, Wisconsin

For information about this book, write or call:

Sheffield Publishing Company
P.O. Box 359
Salem, Wisconsin 53168
(414) 843-2281

Table of Contents

Preface
How It All Started

In my fifteen years as a counselor, I have dealt with people of all ages, ethnic backgrounds, religions, and sexual preference. The one basic cause of their difficulties seemed to stem from their lack of self esteem. Once the problem of low self concept was addressed and the skills learned and practiced to achieve a feeling of strength and confidence, their lives quickly began to be more productive; everything seemed easier.

The same was true in the classes I taught. The New Horizons for Women class, which was tailored to the needs of the reentry woman, dealt first with the women's self concepts. Most of these women came to college frightened and expecting to fail. Each one assumed that she was the least qualified to succeed but wanted so desperately to do well. They needed first to learn to believe in their capacity to do college work. Once they acquired the necessary self esteem, they went on to become outstanding students of the college.

The Stress Management class, as a group, found that many of the stresses they experienced were created because of low self esteem; they were forever agonizing over their weaknesses and their supposed inadequacies. They were constantly worrying about what others were thinking about them and whether they would gain others' approval. When they practiced the steps to gain self esteem and how to keep it, their stress was greatly reduced.

The Eliminating Self-Defeating Behavior class seemed to be made up of generally low-concept people, all with the same need—to learn how to feel better about themselves. Their self-defeating behaviors often were adopted as an escape to their feelings of inferiority. Once those feelings disappeared, their destructive behaviors were extinguished.

And, finally, the Assertive Training class was comprised mostly of individuals who were non-assertive. The primary cause for their unassertive behavior was lack of self esteem. They didn't feel worthy or that they had a right to speak their mind. Hence, we worked on improving their self image before we embarked into learning assertive skills.

In both the individual counseling I do and in the classes I teach, I find that a simple, specific, step-by-step method is needed to find self esteem. People want explicit directions on how to acquire and keep a positive image of themselves. It did no good for me to assure them that they were O.K. or have their classmates give them positive feedback. When people feel inadequate, they are not open to verbal strokes from the outside. They need to feel the warmth of positive thoughts from the *inside; they* speaking to *themselves* in an approving manner. They want a system which they can put into action.

Over the years, I have developed such a method which has proved to be successful when implemented by hundreds of counselees and students. This step-by-step system has also been presented at the many workshops I have conducted on self esteem. I have received comments and letters from those in attendance saying that they have applied these techniques to their lives, and it **has** made a remarkable difference. They have asked me to record these systematic procedures in book form. This book is in response to their requests.

Introduction

It is interesting, and rather amusing, that I would be writing a book which *could* be, and in all probability, *will* be classified as a "self-help" book. At one time, I was not an advocate of self-help books in general. The major reason for this bias was because I have worked with so many people who felt *worse* after reading a self-help publication. It took some time for me to figure out **why.** I have concluded that there are two distinct reasons for those negative reactions. One: the book may have promised the impossible—"If you follow these instructions, all your problems will disappear and your life will be trouble-free and blissful from now on." Persons would read the book in all earnestness; and yet they found that their problems did **not** disappear nor did their lives become trouble-free and blissful. Hence, they were disenchanted and also felt that they had failed to do the things correctly which the book suggested as "cure-alls." This made them feel worse than before they read the book. They felt they had failed again.

The second reason was that the reader of a realistic self-help book (one which does not promise miracles) was just that—a "reader." The reader did nothing to put into practice the methods suggested. Without putting ideas into actions—

thoughts into behaviors—no change can possibly occur! No book can make a difference in your life unless you put the principles suggested into practice. Once you read the words and adopt them for use in your life, then comes the work of transferring ideas into actions. That's the way to have self-help books make a difference. Often the "self" is ignored in "self-help." The author offers the "help"; the "self"—whoever that may be— has to adapt it into his or her life with practice, patience and persistence. None of us would think of reading a book on "How To Keep Fit" and expect to be in top shape without practicing— over and over—the tips offered in the book.

So it is with this book on self esteem. It can show you the ways to get self esteem and keep it; but, it's up to you to follow through with the perfecting of these skills by practicing, being patient with yourself and persistent by practicing, again and again. I sincerely believe this book can be helpful to you. The methods do work. I have seen them change individuals who had no self esteem into confident, happy individuals who now have high self esteem. These "techniques" have been successful for counselees, students in my classes, participants at my workshops; and, most convincing of all, they have worked for **me**! The material included in this book will lead to self esteem, but only if you believe it will work for you and then diligently put it to use in your everyday living. It is necessary to act out these skill-building procedures and keep doing them until they become second-nature.

To assist you in practicing the skills that lead to self esteem, I have prepared **Self Esteem Work Outs** at the end of each chapter. In order to get the most out of this book, it will be to your advantage to do these exercises. It is possible that you could share these activities with friends or family who may wish to join in the fun of achieving self esteem. Remember, you can't become proficient at a skill unless you work at it!

In our society of instant meals, instant entertainment, instant gratifications, we may expect instant change. An internal change takes time and effort, but it can be done. Acquiring self esteem is a skill that **anyone** can learn, but it won't happen over-night. To learn to do anything well takes time and effort; but the rewards will be worth it. To accept oneself—unconditionally, to be happy to be **you,** to be free to be yourself; all these and more will be the by-products of your gaining self esteem! And it's all within your power.

It seems to me that self esteem is harder to come by these days since people are moving at so fast a pace that they don't often take time to say the complimentary things they may be thinking and feeling about one another. They are so preoccupied with their jobs, their problems, their responsibilities, that they don't stop to encourage others. They are so busy climbing to the top, or racing "just to keep up" that they are consumed with their own needs. Therefore, it is even more crucial for you to find out how to depend on yourself for self esteem. If I could give you **one** belief, it would be that **you** are in charge of your self esteem. Everything I will suggest to you for building a positive self image is under your control. There are not many things that we feel (rightly or wrongly) that we have control over. You **can** and **do** have control over your self esteem. **You** can be responsible for feeling relaxed, assertive, capable, independent, accomplished and all the other feelings that come with approving of yourself.

You are in charge of your self esteem—from this moment on. You are the one who will read these words—accept or reject them; and then, put them to use in your life with practice, patience and persistence. The help is here; **you** put it to use!

> *First of all, although men have a common destiny, each individual also has to work out his own personal salvation for himself in fear and trembling. We can help one another to find the meaning of life no doubt. But in the last analysis, the individual person is responsible for living his own life and for "finding himself." If he persists in shifting his responsibility to somebody else, he fails to find out the meaning of his own existence. You cannot tell me who I am, and I cannot tell you who you are. If you do not know your own identity, who is going to identify you?*
>
> **Thomas Merton**

WHAT IS IT?

WHAT IS IT?

YOUR WORLD

POSITIVE CYCLE

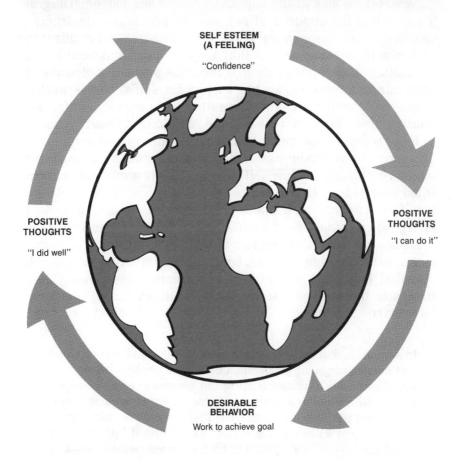

**SELF ESTEEM
(A FEELING)**

"Confidence"

**POSITIVE
THOUGHTS**

"I can do it"

**POSITIVE
THOUGHTS**

"I did well"

**DESIRABLE
BEHAVIOR**

Work to achieve goal

Diagram 1

prefer to use their talents and wit to delight others by being "center stage." There is no commonality or *right way* to behave when you have self esteem. The behaviors are as varied and as different as the individuals who possess a positive self image. We each have our own style. But, the behavior is generally effective, attractive, meaningful, respectable and pleasant to us and to those with whom we interact.

Now, take a look at the negative cycle of self esteem (Diagram Two). It has the opposite effect on your life. It is a destructive, debilitating, demonic cycle! If we become entrapped in this cycle of low self esteem, we *feel* that we are inept, unloveable, and insignificant. Our *thoughts* are negative and self-defeating. In turn, our *behaviors* are hostile, suspicious, selfish, non-assertive, aggressive, withdrawn, procrastinating, unconvincing, and unattractive. Our reactions and the reactions of those around us to these unappealing *behaviors* are often harsh and humiliating. These reactions produce more negative *thoughts* about ourselves which reinforces our **low** self esteem. This is a miserable, unfulfilled way to live. If you are caught in this unhealthy cycle, you can free yourself. It's under your control. Again, **who** is in charge of your feelings, thoughts, and behaviors? **You are!**

Before we leave this chapter of what self esteem is, I'd like to share with you some quotes I have gathered from people who revealed how lack of self esteem affected their lives. I give thanks to these people; from those who have sought my help, I have learned the most.

In school, lack of self esteem makes me nervous and anxious, and causes physical problems, i.e., stomachaches, headaches, etc. I feel I don't measure up to the teachers' expectations. I tend to sit in the back in some classes where I feel inadequate and do not participate. I feel what I have to say is unimportant and everyone will think I'm stupid. Therefore, if I don't understand the lesson or homework, I'll let it pass, which causes a problem later.

The results of lack of self esteem leaves me with an inferiority complex. I allow others to make my decisions. Fear dominates my living — creating excessive nervousness. I am extremely sensitive, and have difficulty in expressing my feelings. Living with these shortcomings is very stressful and really hard to understand or explain.

YOUR WORLD

NEGATIVE CYCLE

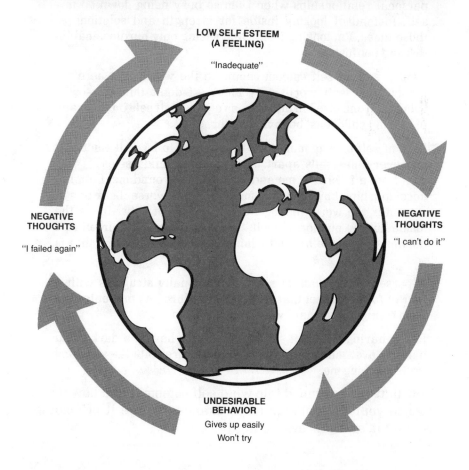

LOW SELF ESTEEM (A FEELING)

"Inadequate"

NEGATIVE THOUGHTS

"I can't do it"

UNDESIRABLE BEHAVIOR

Gives up easily
Won't try

NEGATIVE THOUGHTS

"I failed again"

Diagram 2

Having a lack of self esteem perpetuates the myth that I am no good. It discounts all my goodness and rivets my attention on the mistakes of the past; not seeing them as mistakes, or individual incidents, or as lessons but internalizing them and looking at them as proof of my badness.

Having a lack of self esteem limits me. It is difficult to be open to creative options in problem solving and in effective interpersonal relationships when I am so busy being down on myself. Instead of looking inside for strength and solutions at those times, I'm looking inside and seeing only hurdles, inabilities and confusion.

Having lack of self esteem shouts to the world that here's a person who isn't worth very much—I don't think so—why should anyone else? In my case, as a parent, it sets a bad example for my childrens' behavior patterns.

Lack of self esteem makes me cry. I seem to lose all emotions, and everything falls apart. I feel helpless and useless. I feel as if I am a failure to me and also people around me. I am not accomplishing anything only making things worse. Lack of self esteem is the worst feeling I can have. It not only affects the inside but the outside as well. So you are hurting yourself and hurting the people around who love you and care; and that is sad.

A person with a lack of self esteem usually struggles with a fear of failure. I feel that this fear of failure has prevented me from trying things that I would really like to do.

Really having a lack of self esteem is like having a dark cloud hanging over me most of the time and it prevents the sunshine from reaching me.

Now that you are tuned into what self esteem is and how it can influence your life, let's go on to examine where it originates, how to get it, and how to keep it.

Self Esteem "Work Outs"

1. Choose an example from your life that fits the positive self esteem cycle. Recall, in detail, your feelings, thoughts, and behaviors.

2. Now choose a situation from your life that fits the negative self esteem cycle. Recall, in detail, your feelings, thoughts, and behaviors.

   (a) Which cycle gave you the best feelings?

   (b) You are now in charge of making it a practice to use only the positive cycle. You have control over your feelings, thoughts, and actions.

   (c) Try to become aware when you are functioning in either one of these cycles.

3. Did you identify with any of the persons' quotations who shared how lack of self esteem affected their lives? They learned to feel good about themselves. You can, too!

4. Place a check by the words in columns A and B below that describe your feelings, thoughts, and behaviors most of the time.

A (−)	B (+)
depressed	good — all over
sad	light hearted
helpless	back on top
alone	capable
insecure	beautiful
immobilized	energetic
worthless	happy
self critical	loveable
inactive	friendly
withdrawn	healthy
intimidated	outgoing
confused	useful
idiotic	warm
drained	bubbly
weak	youthful

A (−)	B (+)
angry	cheerful
vulnerable	confident
defensive	secure
weighted down	peaceful
negative	purposeful
aggressive	intelligent
unfriendly	creative
frustrated	satisfied
self-pity	content
moody	receptive
apathetic	vivacious
selfish	successful
sarcastic	thankful
stupid	satiated
hateful	optimistic
humorless	needs are met
anxious	courageous
useless	proud
friendless	ambitious
unloved	loved
unloveable	self-assured
incapable	trustworthy
not needed	fortunate
frightened	self-reliant

(a) In which column do you have the most checks?

(b) Don't be discouraged if you had many more checks in column A than column B. The following chapters will help you move from column A to column B.

5. Become *aware* of how *you* behave when you have high self esteem. You can't alter your behavior from "bad" to "good" unless you are aware of what *your* typical good behavior is. Give yourself strokes for that desirable behavior.

6. Become aware of how you behave when your self esteem is **low.** Realize how destructive that behavior is to you and **stop it!** *You* are in charge of your behavior. Trace back and see what thoughts and feelings you had that precipitated this undesirable behavior. *You* are the controller of your thoughts and feelings.

WHERE DOES IT ORIGINATE?

2

Where Does Self Esteem Originate?

This chapter will not go into too much detail about where self esteem originates as that is the *past*, and one must deal in the present. However, knowing where the seed of your self esteem was first planted and what nurtured its growth is interesting to reflect on. We are always curious to know why we develop as we do; it brings understanding and allows us to escape, for a moment, the responsibility of our own behavior. We will not, however, become stuck in the sands of time, as that immobilizes us and inhibits our growth. So, we will take a nostalgic backward glance and then proceed to the *present* and follow the steps for achieving and maintaining self esteem.

Were you born with self esteem—or the lack of it? No, your feelings about how you fit into the world were awakened by the experiences around you from the time of your birth. Each person has an inner computer which monitored your feelings about yourself before you could either walk or talk. This computer gathered data from the tone of the voices which spoke to you, from the gentleness or harshness of the touches you received, from the amount of attention paid to you, from the reactions to your cries for food—all symbols of love or rejection. Your sensitive computer did the gathering from your exterior world, and **you** interpreted the collected data as either positive or negative input. A preponderance of positive input resulted in your saying to yourself, "I must be O.K.—for that is the message I'm receiving from the world around me." If the input was interpreted as negative, the result was that you felt you didn't quite measure-up and were an inferior individual. Some researchers say that self concept is firmly formed by age seven. That seems rather early; but, as you know, it continues to change and develop throughout our lives. Self esteem is a **learned** feeling that originated from the experiences that you were part of from your first day on earth.

Let's explore the different types of environments which may have had an influence on your self esteem. Perhaps you were raised in one of these environments—or a combination of them. The first one we'll examine is the **positive** environment. In this environment the child is fully accepted and respected as a person. His or her needs and wishes are taken into serious consideration. The parents establish and enforce clearly defined perimeters within which the child performs—definite standards of performance are set up and excellence is rewarded. The parents, themselves, are persons with high levels of self esteem. A great deal of research has been done in recent years to determine what conditions in child rearing lead to helping the child develop high self esteem. The conditions just described seem to be optimum for the child to feel worthwhile, loveable, useful, competent and to lead to a happy, productive life. Chances are, if you were raised in such an atmosphere, your self esteem flourished at an early age.

Next, is the **negative** environment, one in which the inner computer picks up data that is primarily negative. This comes from actions, words and attitudes directed *to* you and *about* you which say that you are stupid, unattractive, hopeless, less-than, unwanted, an encumbrance, and generally a pain! Remarks such as: "Can't you do **anything** right?", "Won't you ever learn?", "How can I put up with you another minute?", "Why can't you be like your sister?", "Can't you do **something** about your appearance?". All these are questions which don't require an answer; they are statements defining inferiority; and they make the recipient feel most unworthy. The inner computer is busily picking up this negative data until this becomes the *primary* language; and, so, it does not respond to the occasional positive input that comes along. Therefore, the interpretation made by the person who receives these "put-downs" is that the comments are true, and that he or she is an inferior person—inadequate and doomed to fail. This is a **learned** process and can be **un**learned. If you were raised in this particular environment, hopefully, you have learned another way to view yourself. **You** are in command now, and you have changed that negative perception dictated by others about you. I am sure you have changed many of your behaviors learned in childhood. You no doubt go to bed and get up at different times than were required when you were young. Your diet has probably changed, and your dinner hours are now set by **you.** You made these changes to accommodate your life style. You can also change the feelings which you had about yourself when you were growing up in that negative atmosphere. You are not stuck with that old belief pattern unless you wish to be!

The third environment is the **perfect** environment; one in which you were convinced daily that everything you did was perfect. All those important others who adored you were constantly telling you that you did everything skillfully—and better than anyone else. You were touted as the prettiest or handsomest, the brightest, the most courageous, the most talented—on and on. Your inner computer was almost overwhelmed picking up all this glowing information. The decision you made from perusing this data was, "Mmmmm, I must be **perfect!**" This leads to an overblown and unrealistic feeling of self esteem which can lead to trouble later on. It's difficult for the persons who received this "perfect" message to enter the real world—outside of this exaggerated environment. They soon find, to their bewilderment, that they are truly **not** perfect. This is deflating to their inflated self image and leaves them questioning whether they can do **anything** right. Or, they could have interpreted the original superlative data to mean they **must** be perfect in order to feel adequate. That, if they do not excel at **everything,** they are not acceptable. That sets up the "dog-chasing-the-tail-syndrome" in self esteem; one can never catch up. Consequently, they always feel frustrated and unfulfilled. Those feelings, too, can be changed. It's never too late when you realize that now **you** are in charge!

The fourth environment is the **contradictory** environment. That is one in which one parent compliments, overprotects, smothers the child with love and affection every minute. The second parent (perhaps trying to offset the other's overindulgence) is very critical and demanding of the child. From this parent's attitude, you feel you never quite succeed; that, no matter how hard you try, you will never completely please or make that parent proud of you. It is a confusing and "no win" experience—day after day. One time you are told you are superlative; the next time you're berated for being stupid. The inner computer picks up a positive bit of information from the first parent which is quickly contradicted and canceled out by the second parent's input. This leaves the computer empty or with a confused question mark. You are left with "fluctuating self esteem"; that is, you are never quite sure how you feel about yourself from one experience to the next. That's unsettling; it stops you from being productive or from taking many risks. That anxious, tentative feeling can be changed to a confident, determined, sure, optimistic one. That confusing message can be overcome and you can be transformed into a clear, positive one—by **you**. You are in control now.

Some people, who feel that their low self concept came from their childhood, continue to blame, resent, even hate those whom they consider responsible. This is non-productive; it does nothing to change the situation. That attitude won't allow you to find self esteem. I feel sure that parents did the best job of raising you they could. Why let the negative influences continue to have power over you? It is time to forgive and forget and get on with building your own self esteem. The only purpose in looking back is to understand better. Then, one must go about the business of changing—improving—achieving—knowing that now **you** are the master of your feelings. If not you, then who? As Eleanor Roosevelt said, "No one can make you feel inferior without your permission." So, **stop** being a "victim"; it isn't necessary if you take control of your life.

I propose, first, that you take charge of your inner computer. Stop the mindless, indiscriminate collection of positive and negative data from people around you. Instead, **you** carefully consider each item of feedback that you receive. If there is negative input, judge whether it is valid or not (according to **your** value system) and whether it is constructive criticism which can be useful to you. If not, throw it out—don't store it. When you receive positive input, accept it if it fits into what you know to be true about yourself; or enjoy the warmth of the moment and hold onto it as a possibility for what you may become.

Next, try to ween yourself away from depending on others for your self esteem. Apart from the opinions of a few significant others, what people say or think of you is largely irrelevant. It's true; think about it.

If you are constantly depending on others to determine how you feel about yourself, you are in for a frustrating life. You have lost control; you are like a yo-yo being managed by others. We are all different; our values are different; our frames of reference are different. Therefore, how do you expect to please **everyone** in order to validate yourself? That's a lost cause. Haven't you changed your hairstyle at some time and the first person whom you meet says, "Oh, what a dynamite hairstyle; I love it! It's so much more becoming than your old one." If you are in the "yo-yo-stage-of-self-esteem," you are pleased with yourself and feel happy. Then, you meet another friend who comments, "Mmmm, that's a new hairstyle, isn't it? It's neat, but I like the other style so much better. It suited you—made you look unique." There you are—swinging like a yo-yo between the comments of two friends. The point is: you will never be at peace with yourself if you are depending on anyone else for your self esteem. It puts you at the mercy of *everyone's* judgement instead of your own. That doesn't mean you won't ask for advice and the opinion of others; but, when you receive it, weigh it according to your perceptions and then make **your own decision.** You are the dominator of your self esteem. It is immature and demeaning behavior to persist in looking to others for establishing a good feeling about yourself. So, if you have made the determination to be responsible for your self esteem, let's proceed with the steps to achieve it!

As the laws of Manu say, "Depend not on another, but lean instead on thyself...True happiness is born of self-reliance...".

Origin "Work Outs"

1. Did your early self concept relate to any of the four environments described in this chapter? Which ones?

2. Has your self esteem changed since you were a child? How?

3. Think of a person from your past who loved you, nurtured you, encouraged you, appreciated you and had a great deal to do with your feeling good about yourself.

    (a) Have you told that person lately how important they were to you?

4. Do you have a person in your life whom you love, encourage, care for, and sustain?

    (a) If so, have you had contact with them lately? They need you; you make a difference in how they feel about themselves.

5. Are you still blaming others for your low self image?

    (a) If so, try to forgive them. Those feelings are destructive to you and are blocking you from taking the responsibility that is yours.

6. Are you leaning on others to give you self esteem?

    (a) If you are, you are in for a frantic life. It's impossible to acquire the approval of **all**, so you will feel you have failed; and your self esteem becomes weak and withers.

    (b) Take the healthy, independent approach—regulate your own feelings...

HOW DO YOU GET IT?

> *"The greatest discovery of my generation is that human beings can alter their lives by altering their attitudes of mind."*
>
> **William James**

3

Your Attitude

We looked into the past to see where your self esteem originated. So much for the *past*; let's deal with the *present* and your self esteem. What can you do about improving your self image **now**? Today is yours to make it whatever you want it to be.

The first, and perhaps the most important step in reaching high self esteem, is **to have a positive attitude!** *You* are in control of your attitude, so that should be easy. Let's check yours. Do you spend an inordinate amount of time thinking about your weaknesses? Do you magnify every little flaw—remember every mistake? Are your sleepless nights filled with worrying about your "stupid" behaviors or things you wish you hadn't said? Are you your own worst critic? If you answered "yes" to any of these questions, that means your attitude needs altering in order to find self esteem.

There are three ways to overhaul your attitude: (1) **concentrate on your strengths,** (2) **don't try to be perfect** and (3) **stop negative mind-feeding.**

The number one way to change your attitude is to turn it around full circle and focus on your **strengths.** Self esteem is discovered by "zooming in" on strengths—not weaknesses. We can't feel good about ourselves if we constantly concentrate on

21

how inadequate we are—or are forever viewing our frailties with dismay. That's a waste of time, and it's demoralizing. It gets you back into that disagreeable *negative-self-esteem-cycle.* Don't do that to your unique and precious self. Everyone has limitations.

There are some common attitudes which deter people from recognizing and using their strengths. People who have "anti-strength" attitudes are divided into two groups: the **"deniers"** and the **"critical comparers."**

The **deniers** are those who deny that they have any strengths. In my years of working with people who have low self esteem, I have yet to encounter a healthy personality who honestly believes that they have **no** strengths. They don't admit the fact that they are skilled to anyone else, but *they* know it. It may be that they feel that their qualities are not recognized or appreciated by others, but *they* know they have them. It takes time for them to see the advantage of bringing these hidden talents "out of the closet." Once they realize that they must nurture and exercise their skills—be thankful they have them— then, chances are, others will begin to value them, also. But, until that time, they may deny the fact that they have any strengths to you and me.

Some **deniers** adopt this attitude to get attention. Their typical pattern of communicating with friends goes like this: "Oh, I don't *have* any talent—I can't do *anything* well." The awaited response is quick to come from the friend, "That's not true. You're the finest _____ I know. You do **many** things well!" This is the "fishing-for-a-compliment manipulation." It conjures up the desired verbal response, but it leaves the recipient empty as before—perhaps even more lacking in self esteem because they feel this is the only way they can get others to emit approval. **Deniers** keep themselves in this behavior bind.

The last category of **deniers** are those who refuse to claim any talent or ability because they wish to avoid responsibility. Their thinking is: "If people *know* I can do such-and-such, I will *have* to do it!" So, they deny that they can do anything. How unproductive and injurious to self esteem. They gain only the feeling that they are good at avoiding responsibility—not a very gratifying goal.

The **critical comparer's** favorite phrase is: "I can do that, **but.**" This group admits they have *some* competence, but won't admit they do anything well; because they insist on comparing themselves to those who do better than they. Examples: "Yes, I have a good singing voice **but** not as lovely as Cleo Laine or Leontyne Price." "I can play tennis **but** not as well as Jimmy Connors." Consistently matching talents with the pros is bound to inhibit the freedom to be pleased with *any* of your strengths. Don't do that!

I have a friend who is a talented artist—makes her living painting and likes what she's doing. She isn't constantly comparing herself to Winslow Homer or Andrew Wyeth and feeling that she doesn't measure up to *their* excellence. That would be self-defeating. Instead, she strives to paint as well as *she* can and congratulates herself when she improves. This is the way to build self esteem.

The other segment of **critical comparers** are assiduously critical of themselves if they don't perform at their **top** level every time. Some say that they employ this attitude in order to motivate themselves to do better the next time. This technique may work for those who have high self esteem. It is not a healthy approach for those who have little self esteem. This flagellating of oneself takes energy; energy that could be used for approving of their strengths. It exerts terrible pressure and can be a form of self-torture. This is no way to develop your potential.

Chris Evert Lloyd, after winning her fifth consecutive French Open Tennis Championship, reflected that she hadn't played up to her top form until the final match. She mused, "But I **did** play very well today!" She didn't fasten her attention on her weaker days; but, rather, spoke with pride to millions of T.V. viewers about her fine tennis that day. Those statements and feelings boosted her self esteem as she practiced for Wimbeldon which followed shortly.

So take yourself out of the **denier** or the **critical comparer** groups and become an **appreciator**! If you are a good cook, mechanic, artist, athlete, student, bread winner, lover or friend—why get upset if you have no particular talent for public speaking, music, sewing or carpentry work? Most of us aren't experts at anything. But you *can* be the best you can be; nobody else can do *that*! The way to self esteem is **not** to compare yourself to the experts in every area but to develop the potential that is yours alone. Your attitude will be: "I'm going to give to the world the best me I can be!" And, then, appreciate your successes. To withhold from yourself the pleasure of rejoicing at your success is to be a hypocrite and a denier of your own happiness.

Find the things that you do well (compared to **you**) and build on these strengths. You have many talents and abilities; just start appreciating them. Often we take our strengths for granted with the attitude that "anybody can do that." I had a woman in my office recently who told me that she was in her twenties before she was aware that her capability to make her own clothes—and without a pattern—was something special. She hadn't acknowledged that skill and talent, because she took it for granted. We dislike other people taking us for granted, but we do it to ourselves much too often.

Think of the things you know—deep down in your heart—that you do well. You know yourself better than anyone else does. You know the kindnesses you've done, the things you've accomplished, the bad habits you've overcome, and the successes you've had. Those are just **some** of your strengths.

William James once estimated that a healthy human being functions at less than 10% of his capacity. Margaret Mead quoted a 6% figure. So, use the best of those percentage capacities to build on, and that will awaken the rest of your unused raw material. It's all in how you view yourself; adopt the attitude that you have much to offer and then start working on developing your strong points.

Are you convinced yet that you should look to your **strengths**? All right, list the individuals whom you admire. One may be a certain T.V. or movie star, a professional athlete, a politician, a writer, a composer, or your neighbor down the street. Whoever it is, take a look at **why** they are "special," and you'll find that they have concentrated on and developed what they do well. Thomas Edison said, "If we all did the thing we are capable of doing, we would astound ourselves." He knew what he was talking about. His inventions evolved from his having the attitude that he **could** do it by building on his strengths. Now all of us can't be a Thomas Edison, but we have our own special strengths which will lie dormant if we don't exercise and expand them to the fullest.

Let's get started with attitude change. Jot down a list of your strengths...Is that difficult? If so, it's not because you don't *have* many strengths. It's probably because this is a new way for you to view yourself. It may even be distasteful for you to do at first, because we've been taught not to dwell on our outstanding qualities. We have been socialized to believe that we must be "humble"—never brag. I'm not suggesting that you become a braggart. Braggarts don't have self esteem. That's why they feel compelled to announce how wonderful they are constantly—hoping that someone will believe what they themselves do not believe. Rather, I am encouraging you, **you by yourself,** to review, accept, take pleasure in and build up your strengths. Dag Hammarskjold stated that "maturity: among other things—is not to hide one's strength out of fear, and, consequently, live below one's best." It is much more productive to think about what we do well, than to ruminate on the mistakes we've made. We all commit errors—even the professionals. I watched Jack Nicklaus miss a four foot putt recently; he then went on to win that tournament. When he was interviewed after the match, he emphasized that he had to put that bad putt out of his mind and go on to the next hole with confidence—thinking about the good strokes and what he was capable of doing at his best.

So, do as the pros do—capitalize on your strengths. Begin to be aware of what you do well. Reward yourself for it; even if it's merely to take time to say to yourself, "That was terrific!", "Best I've ever done," "I've improved a lot over the past week!". Get in touch with the best parts of you and develop them by appreciating them. That's the way to high self esteem. And it's all within your power to bring it about.

Think about what you do well. Think of the positive comments people have made about you. Think about your past successes. Write down some of the things that come into your mind. Here are some samples of activities that people feel good about. "I'm a good: driver, clipper-of-bushes, organizer, shopper, singer, cleaner, dancer, provider, cook, lover, student, friend, listener, exerciser, fire builder, wood chopper, letter writer, fish cleaner, horseback rider, dresser, marksman, giver, seamstress, thinker, speaker, inventor, supporter." There are hundreds more.... Practice bringing to mind the things you are good at. It's that kind of practicing you should do to alter that old "nit-picking" attitude which looks in on the weaknesses and not the strengths. If you find yourself slipping back into the old habit of exaggerating your faults or discounting your strengths, say **stop** and switch gears to give closer attention to your power points. Start being a supporter of yourself; without **your** support, you can't do *any-thing!* Start believing in **you.** Be persistent about this attitude-exercise. Do it several times a day. When you are stopped in traffic, use that waiting period to recount the things you've done well that day. Nurture your self concept with affirmative input so that it will become high self esteem. Remember Diagram One. When you *feel* good about yourself, you will *think* good thoughts, you will *behave* in a pleasant manner. That, in turn, will cause you and others to appreciate and enjoy you. That will make you feel even *better* about yourself—and so on. Be aware of your **strengths** and stop amplifying your weaknesses. That's the first step to controlling your attitude and heading for that wonderful, incomparable feeling of high self esteem!

"Every adult needs a rock, a ground, for his identity — something he knows, something he can do no matter what. For me, the ground is this: I am a psychoanalyst."

Eric Erikson

Strength "Work Outs"

1. Make it a habit, when you are waiting for someone, to review the good things you've done that past week. Translate those actions into **strengths.** Example: "I handed in an important report today. The strengths it took to do that were: organization, ability to write concisely, persistence to get the job done, a facility with data, ability to analyze and crystalize the pertinent points, etc."

2. List the successes you've had in your life.

   (a) Identify the strengths it took to accomplish these successes.

3. List the improvements you've made in yourself over the years.

   (a) Identify the strengths it took to accomplish these improvements.

4. Think about your dreams of the future.

   (a) What strengths can you employ to make this dream a reality?

5. What are you doing **now** to develop the **best parts** of you?

6. Ask a close friend, relative, or spouse to write down your strengths and give you the list.

   (a) Does their assessment of your strengths match yours?

   (b) Do they see strengths in you that you have overlooked? Start appreciating yourself for those strengths, too!

7. What one achievement in your life are you most proud of?

   (a) What strengths did you use to achieve this?

8. Make a list of self-congratulatory statements that you can refer to *often.* Keep adding to this list. (Examples: "Good job," "Nice going," "I'm improving," "Marvelous," "That's the way to go," "What an outstanding effort!", etc.)

9. Get into the habit of giving yourself mental strokes *immediately* following the event in which you did well.

10. Place a tiny colored dot on your watch band. Each time you look at your watch and see the dot, name one of your strengths.

11. At the end of the day, list what you feel good about doing that day.

12. If you awaken in the night and start to worry—change the worry to productive action plans using your strengths.

13. Do "My Winning Strengths" exercise.

My Winning Strengths

Step 1: Put a check (✓) beside each word or phrase that describes you, whether it is all the time or just part of the time. If you have difficulty seeing positive descriptions of yourself, imagine a close friend describing you.

Step 2: After checking your strength words, look at the number that goes with each word. Make a tally mark on the tally list at the top of page 30 for each time you checked a word for that given number.

Strength Word List

9 romantic	13 investing	9 serene	4 prudent
13 busy	8 strong-willed	7 organizer	8 confident
3 kind	16 motivated	14 tactful	16 tireless
9 artistic	3 understanding	10 committed	13 industrious
4 careful	11 disciplined	15 spontaneous	3 thoughtful
13 convincing	8 self-reliant	7 commanding	9 expressive
3 friendly	16 persistent	14 tolerant	4 settled
9 gentle	6 neat	10 goal-directed	13 persuasive
4 loyal	12 caring	15 progressive	3 affectionate
5 distinctive	2 thinker	5 sharp	9 graceful
11 perfectionist	1 clever	11 capable	4 reliable
8 self-determined	6 exact	8 certain	7 leader
16 tenacious	2 well-informed	5 looked up to	10 growing
5 dignified	1 creative	11 dedicated	14 eager
11 ambitious	6 orderly	8 courageous	15 active
8 individualistic	2 outgoing	16 consistent	13 influential
16 steadfast	2 searching	5 honorable	3 giving
5 poised	1 original	11 productive	9 appreciative
16 strong	7 fair-minded	8 determined	4 thrifty
14 considerate	5 respected	7 planner	14 unselfish
10 fulfilled	15 flexible	11 efficient	10 self-aware
15 likes new ideas	7 manager	14 cooperative	10 self-directed
15 open-minded	7 forceful	14 dependable	10 adjusted
1 talented	2 inquiring	12 comforting	6 predictable
1 witty	2 intelligent	12 sociable	6 practical
6 systematic	12 encouraging	2 curious	1 unique
12 trustworthy	1 imaginative	15 adaptable	6 precise
4 foresight	13 pursuing	3 forgiving	12 listener

1. _____   5. _____   9. _____   13. _____

2. _____   6. _____   10. _____   14. _____

3. _____   7. _____   11. _____   15. _____

4. _____   8. _____   12. _____   16. _____

Using those numbers, you can convert the strengths into strength values:

1 = creativity	2 = knowledge	3 = relating	4 = security
5 = prestige	6 = order	7 = leadership	8 = independence
9 = beauty	10 = self-realization	11 = achievement	12 = social service
13 = economic reward	14 = cooperation	15 = variety	16 = endurance

Write the five strength values that have the highest number of marks below:

Strength Values:

14. *Look over* "Some Strengths You May Have Overlooked."
    (a) Add to your strength list.

Some Strengths You May Have Overlooked*

1. **Special Aptitudes or Resources:** Having hunches or making guesses which usually turn out right; following through on these. Having a "green thumb." Mechanical ability, sales ability, ability in mathematics, skill with hands in constructing or repairing things.

2. **Intellectual Strengths:** Applying reasoning ability to problem solving. Intellectual curiosity. Thinking out ideas and expressing them aloud or in writing. Being able to accept new ideas. Doing original or creative thinking. Having the ability to learn and enjoy learning.

3. **Education, Training, and Related Areas:** All education beyond grade school, including high school, college, advanced study, vocational training, on-the-job training, special courses you have taken, and self-education through study and organized reading. Any high grades. Any scholastic and related honors.

4. **Work, Vocation, Job or Position:** Includes years of experience in a particular line of work, as well as having successfully held different positions in different lines. Having held a responsible or supervisory position. Owning or managing your own full-time or part-time enterprise. Job satisfaction, including enjoying your work, good relations with co-workers, feelings of loyalty toward employer or organization, pride in work and duties.

5. **Aesthetic Strengths:** Recognizing and enjoying beauty in nature, the arts, or people, and as expressed through the personality of people. Using aesthetic sense to enhance home and physical environment.

6. **Organizational Strengths:** Developing and planning sensible short-range and long-range goals. Carrying out orders, as well as giving them. Experience in organizing enterprises, projects, clubs—social, political, or other. Having held leadership positions in such organizations.

---

*"Some Strengths You May Have Overlooked," from *Group Methods to Actualize Human Potential Handbook* by Herbert Otto, The Holistic Press, 1970.

7. **Hobbies and Crafts:** All hobbies, crafts, and related interests, including any instruction or training in such crafts as weaving, pottery, and jewelry making. Any other interests to which you give time.

8. **Expressive Arts:** Any type of dancing. Any form of writing (stories, essays, poetry). Sketching, painting, sculpture, modeling with clay. Ability to improvise music or to play a musical instrument, definite rhythmic ability and so forth.

9. **Health:** Good health represents a strength. List any measures for maintaining or improving your health, including seeking adequate medical treatment at once when needed, yearly medical check-ups, and any other means designed for this purpose.

10. **Sports and Outdoor Activities:** Active participation in outdoor activities and organized sports, camping, hunting. Regular exercise programs.

11. **Imaginative and Creative Strengths:** Using creativity and imagination for new and different ideas in relation to home, family, job or vocation. Working on developing and extending your imagination and creative abilities.

12. **Relationship Strengths:** Ability to meet people easily, make them feel comfortable, ability to talk freely with strangers. Good relations with neighbors. Treating people with consideration, politeness, and respect at all times. Being aware of the needs and feelings of others. Being able to really listen to what others have to say. Helping others to be aware of their strengths and abilities as well as their shortcomings or problems. Relating to people as individuals, regardless of sex, creed or race. Giving people the feeling that you understand them.

13. **Emotional Strengths:** Ability to give as well as to receive affection or love. Being able to feel a wide range of emotions. Being able to do or express things on the spur of the moment. Ability to "put yourself in the other fellow's shoes," to feel what he feels. Understanding the role of your feelings and emotions in every day of living.

14. **Other Strengths:** Humor as a source of strength—being able to laugh at yourself and to take kidding at your own expense. Liking to adventure or pioneer, to explore new horizons or

try new ways. Ability to stick your neck out, to risk yourself with people and in situations.

Perseverance or stick-to-it-iveness; having a strong drive to get things done and doing them.

Ability to manage finances, evidenced by investments and savings, among other things.

Knowledge of languages or of different peoples and cultures, through travel, study, or reading.

Making the best of your appearance by means of grooming and good choice of clothes.

"Think of what you have rather than of what you lack. Of the things you have, select the best and then reflect how eagerly you would have sought them if you did not have them."

Marcus Aurelius

Nobody's Perfect

The second part of "attitude control" is **not to expect yourself to be perfect!** If your attitude is one of perfectionism—that of setting extremely high standards and being displeased with anything else—you will find it difficult to have self esteem. Trying to be perfect allows you to have only **conditional-tentative** self esteem. **Conditional,** because your benevolent feelings about yourself are conditional on your performing *perfectly.* You feel you don't measure up unless you are perfect. **Tentative,** because perfectionism bleeds into everything you do. You not only expect to be perfect at one or two activities—but **all** of them! Therefore, you are satisfied only momentarily (if at all); and, then, on to the next impossible goal. That's setting one's self up for failure and the elimination of self esteem. What an anxious, disappointing, frustrating, exhausting life a perfectionist lives.

Lois is a good example of leading this kind of life. She is a reentry woman at college. She came to me completely frustrated and exhausted. She felt she was a failure. She was trying to be perfect in everything. Her house was spotless; she was ready to entertain her husband's business associates at the drop of a hat; she was the "number one" roommother for both of her children at school; she was a perfect daughter to her elderly parents who demanded much of her time; she was getting excellent grades in her college courses; her appearance was impeccable; she saw that her husband's and children's clothes were in perfect condition...No wonder she was tired out and ready to withdraw from college. She was a victim of her own perceptions; she felt she must be perfect in everything.

Lois learned to prioritize her activities and not to expect that each one be done **perfectly.** She allowed herself the right to be wrong occasionally. Her life improved; her self esteem returned, and she stayed in school.

You might say, "That's all very well for Lois, but I was always expected to be perfect as a child; it's a habit I can't break. I can't help it." **Wrong.....** You are in charge of your attitude; you *can* break that pattern if you want to. Much of our misery in this life is caused by unrealistic expectations of ourselves and others. If your expectations of yourself require that you must be perfect, *that's* what's wrong—your attitude—not your imperfections.

Change your attitude by being kind to yourself. You undoubtedly don't expect perfection of others; why give yourself that impossible assignment? If "being perfect" is part of your value system, scratch it off **now** if you ever want to feel the comfort of self esteem. How can you think well of yourself if you are constantly falling short of your goals? And, how can you not fall short if you are expecting perpetual perfection? Self esteem arises from accomplishing what matches the truth about our own possibilities.

You may protest that you are not trying to be perfect for yourself; (you know you make mistakes), but you are trying to be perfect in other people's eyes. That, too, is an invalid attitude. There are several reasons why you can't be seen by others as perfect. First of all, there are *some* folks who won't like *anything* you do—no matter what! If you **could** be perfect, they'd still find something wrong.

Secondly, everyone has a different value system and different standards for perfection. "You can't please all of the people—all of the time." For instance, have you ever prepared a variation of an old favorite dish and served it to your family? One member might say, "Wow, this is delicious. You added something different. I love it!" From another "not-so-eager-eater" at the table might come, "It's O.K., but **why** change a perfect recipe? I like the old one much better." Different people have different palates for perfection.

Or, maybe you've worked hard all week practicing on your golf swing to improve your form. That weekend, you tee off with the usual foursome. One of your opponents notices the "improvement" and comments favorably on it. Your partner takes you aside on the next tee and whispers, "That 'tricky John' is trying to beat us psychologically again. That's no improvement in your stroke. You're not following through on your shots as you usually do. It's taking 25 yards off your woods. Go back to your old swing." That's really different strokes for different folks! You can't be perfect in other people's eyes; they're all individuals with individual rating systems for perfection.

Then, if you are trying to "make points" with friends by being perfect, it usually works the other way. Perfectionists are not pleasant to be with; they often become surly and cross when they aren't succeeding (doing something *perfectly*). Have you ever played tennis with a perfectionist? When they lose a point, they verbally abuse themselves. When they net a serve, they sulk. They are so concerned about their perfect performance that they haven't much time to comment on *your* ace or *your* beautiful backhand. They are self-centered. It is as if they were playing against themselves; that's a no-win match...You undoubtedly will find another tennis companion the next time you play.

Perfectionists are viewed as boring, predictable, untouchable, unconcerned about others. In other words, **no fun**!

Being a perfectionist is a miserable life—for you—and for those around you. Allow yourself the privilege of making a mistake. We all like people who can laugh at themselves rather than taking themselves so seriously. Often the perfectionist's first impulse when something goes wrong is to blame someone else for the error. Their self esteem is so shaky that they want to transfer the blame to others. It's not pleasant to be on the receiving end of that blame.

So, being perfect in other people's eyes is impossible and doesn't make one comfortable to be with.

Perfectionists retard their own growth. Growth comes from risking—trying something new and mastering it. Often perfectionists try something **once**; if they don't excel immediately, they become impatient, discouraged, and give it up without a fair trial. That is stunting to a full, well-rounded life. Enjoy activities for the sake of being with friends, communing with nature, getting exercise, learning something new—rather than setting up perfection as your goal.

A perfectionistic attitude does not lead to being productive. David Burns, M.D., and author of *Feeling Good: The New Mood Therapy*, administered a questionnaire that measured perfectionistic attitudes to a group of 34 highly successful insurance agents at the Philadelphia Million Dollar Forum. The salaries of the group ranged from $29,000 a year to more than $250,000. Eighteen of the agents proved to have perfectionistic ways of thinking, while 16 were nonperfectionistic. He also administered a second questionnaire that assessed the tendency to measure personal worth and self esteem by success and productivity. He anticipated that the highest salaries would be earned by those who were perfectionistic and most likely to evaluate their self esteem in terms of sales.

To his surprise, the average earnings of the perfectionists were not significantly greater than those of the nonperfectionists. In fact, the trend was in the opposite direction; the perfectionists who linked self-worth and achievement earned an average of $15,000 a year **less** than the nonperfectionists did. Apparently, the salesmen who were striving for perfection were actually paying a price in dollars for their mental habit. This shows that productivity is stinted by the attitude of perfectionism. Perfectionists generally experience more punishment than reward.

Perfectionists never give themselves the luxury of basking in the success of improvement. We need those pleasant plateaus where we can wallow in our achievements before taking the next step. We need times like that to store up fodder for our self esteem building in preparation for the bad times. None of us can glide through life with a full sail of self esteem every minute. There will be rough times for all of us; and, at times like these, we need to have a reservoir of positive memories of the things we've done well. Perfectionists don't have this reservoir from which to draw. They don't recognize improvement as a success, because it isn't absolutely perfect. Or, they are on to the next anxious attempt at perfection—never stopping to luxuriate in their accomplishment at that time.

How long would a professional baseball player last if he expected a home run every time he came up to bat? Or a woman golf professional who was devastated if she didn't shoot par or birdie every hole? Or a fisherperson who considered it a tragedy if he or she didn't catch the limit on each outing?

Now, that doesn't mean that we shouldn't strive for improvement or continue to grow. That's a different story; we all understand that forward movement is necessary. But, perfectionism is not a realistic attitude to have; and it's a sure inhibitor for self esteem.

Don't live under the pressure of perfectionism unless you want only **"conditional-tentative"** self esteem. Accept the fact that nobody's perfect—not even you. Change your attitude. You can do it. It will be worth it; you'll feel that wonderful glow inside which is self esteem!

Perfectionist's "Work Outs"

1. Do you demand that you be perfect at your job and/or your leisure time activities?
   (a) How might you change that attitude?
   (b) If you wish, share these attempted changes with a loving friend and have them monitor your behavior.

2. Have you laughed at yourself lately when you did something foolish?
   (a) If you answered, "yes," you might share your "goof" with someone who loves you.

3. Did you improve at something lately?
   (a) Take time to feel good about yourself.
   (b) Reward yourself for that improvement.

4. **Are you a perfectionist?** If you're not sure whether or not you suffer from perfectionism, you may want to test yourself. This can be done by deciding how much you agree with the following statements. Give yourself a + 20 if you agree; a + 10 if you agree somewhat; a 0 if you feel neutral; a – 10 if you disagree slightly; a – 20 if you disagree strongly. Use the number which indicates how you feel about the statement most of the time. Choose only one answer for each statement.

_____ 1. If I make a mistake, people will think I'm stupid.

_____ 2. I should never make the same mistake twice.

_____ 3. I'm a second-class person if I don't have *high* standards.

_____ 4. I should excel at anything I really work at.

_____ 5. I can't be satisfied with an average performance.

_____ 6. If I fail at something important, I dislike myself.

_____ 7. If I don't do well at something, I should give it up.

_____ 8. If I don't live up to my expectations, a good self-scolding will help me improve the next time.

_____ 9. It is wrong for me to show weakness or act foolishly.

_____ 10. If I make a mistake, I *should* be unhappy with myself.

Scoring: Add up your scores on all items. Note that plus numbers and minus numbers cancel each other. For example, if your answer on five items was + 10 and your score on the other five was – 10, your total score would be 0. If you answered + 20 on all items, your total score would be + 200, showing a high degree of perfectionism. If you answered – 20 on every item, your total score of – 200 would signify a strongly nonperfectionist mindset. Studies have shown that about half of the population is apt to score from + 20 to + 160, which indicates varying degrees of perfectionism.

How did you rate?

5. Have you "risked" lately? Give an example.
   (a) As Darlene Berent says, "Don't be afraid to take risks. Even when you lose, you learn so much from the failure that the risk is worth it."

6. Share with a friend, spouse, or family member the advantages of changing your perfectionistic attitude. **Be specific.**

7. Some thoughts to keep in mind that counteract the need to be perfect:
   (a) I would like to do my best with this effort, but I do not *have* to be perfect.
   (b) I'm still an O.K. person even when I make a mistake.
   (c) I can do something well and appreciate it without its being perfect.
   (d) I will be happier and perform better if I try to work at a realistic level rather than demanding perfection of myself.

(e) It is impossible for anyone to function perfectly every time.

Until these thoughts get to be second nature, pin them up where you can refer to them often.

5

Negative Mind-Feeding

*"Man is the only animal endowed with
the capacity to make himself miserable."*

The third part of having a positive attitude is to **stop your negative mind-feeding!** By that, I mean eliminate the catastrophic, illogical, self-defeating, negative thoughts you have about yourself. We all engage in this self-destructive habit. For some, **negative mind-feeding** is so habitual that it isn't even noticed. This leads to misperceiving reality, creating unnecessary distance and conflict between ourselves and others, preventing our accomplishing goals, and, most important, destroying self esteem.

We would never intentionally serve ourselves tainted food, but we feed our minds "garbage" quite often. And, we believe it! How gullible we are to our own thoughts. Before we believe negative statements made by others, we sift the data, check the information to be sure it's correct, and analyze it all with precision. Not so with our negative mind-feeding; we accept as the truth whatever we tell ourselves — without checking further.

An example: You ask a friend to lunch. She refuses. Says she's sorry, but she has other plans. **Your negative mind-feeding**

begins: "Busy with what? She just doesn't want to be with me. Thinks I'm boring. Doesn't like the way I dress. Doesn't want to be seen with me in public. She never invites me anyplace. She owes me a dinner. I'll be darned if I'll call her again until she calls me!" **Your actions** the next time you have a conversation with her are distant, uncommunicative, chip-on-the-shoulder. **The truth of the situation:** She was really busy and very sorry that she couldn't join you for lunch. So, your unpleasant actions may lead to her being annoyed. All because of your negative mind-feeding that had no basis whatsoever!

Another example: You invite a fellow to dinner. He doesn't eat much—picks at the food, but he compliments you on your cooking. **Your negative mind-feeding begins:** "Hah, a good cook? He's hardly eaten a bite. He doesn't like my cooking. Why did he say he did? He's not sincere. He surely won't come back here to eat. He probably won't ask me out again. Guess that's the end of our relationship. All over my poor cooking. That's silly. If he really cared about me, he'd overlook the fact that I'm a lousy cook. Guess that lets me know how he really feels about me. So much for *him!*"

Your attitude the next time he calls: cold and defensive— seemingly disinterested. **The truth of the situation:** He wasn't feeling well. He did like the food but couldn't eat much at the time. He didn't want to break the date for dinner because of illness, because he liked so much to be with you. Hated to miss a chance to be in your presence—even for an evening. Your negative mind-feeding may have ruined your relationship.

Those are just two examples of how negative mind-feeding can interfere with your personal life and do a great deal of damage to your self esteem.

Albert Ellis, Rational Emotive therapist, espouses the theory that feelings (like the feeling of self esteem) are reactions to thoughts, which are reactions to situations. He uses the ABC's to illustrate this. "A" is the activating event: "C" is your feelings and behaviors which we often contribute to the activating event. This is a mistaken belief. What happens between "A" and "C"? **Your thoughts** are "B." You have inner conversations with yourself; these inner dialogues occur at point "B" of the ABC's. If these thoughts are irrational and negative about yourself, your feeling of self esteem is **gone** at point "C."

Fallacy: "A"------presumably leads directly to------"C"

(activating   (your feelings
event)   and behaviors)

Reality: "A"-----leads to---"B"---which lead to-----"C"

(activating   (your   (your feelings
event)   thoughts)   and behaviors)

To further demonstrate this point, the same activating event can happen to two people, and their feelings and behaviors following this event can be entirely different. The difference in their attitudes is caused by their thoughts concerning the activating event.

For example: Beth and Jane are walking down the corridor in an office building. They meet their immediate supervisor. The supervisor is usually warm and friendly; but, on this occasion, he passes the women without a glance. That's the activating event. Jane thinks nothing of it and goes on with her conversation about the happenings of the day. Beth feels worried, puzzled, anxious and wonders what **she** could have done to offend her boss. Same activating event—but entirely different behaviors and feelings. Why? Because of the thoughts Beth had as opposed to Jane's thoughts. Jane observed the difference in the supervisor's actions but sloughed it off by thinking "Mmmm, Bill must be having a bad day; he seemed preoccupied." Beth's negative mind-feeding, on the other hand, may have gone something like this: "My, that's unusual behavior for Mr. Archer, he usually smiles and stops to chat when he meets me. I wonder what I could have done to displease him? Maybe that report I prepared wasn't up to his standards. I just couldn't seem to gather the information he wanted. Seems that I've been slipping lately in my work. I have trouble keeping up. Maybe I'm not as bright or as qualified as the others in the office. Do you suppose they're considering firing me?" and on and on with the irrational negative mind-feeding. This will result in feelings of stress, insecurity, anger and *lack of self esteem*. A simple situation has been escalated into a major catastrophe.

The locus of control is in our heads—not in external events. If you speak to yourself in insulting and derogatory terms, you aren't going to think well of yourself. That isn't the climate that encourages self esteem. We don't always have control over the events in our lives; but we **do** have control over our thoughts; and, therefore, our feelings and behaviors. So, this is another part of your attitude which you can regulate in order to build self esteem.

The last illustration showed how the same activating event can induce an entirely different outcome of feelings and behaviors in two people, because their thoughts about that event were different. Now, let's consider what can happen when just one person is involved.

Ed's family is off on a shopping spree; he has chosen to stay home and work on his car. It had been malfunctioning; and he's decided to take this time, when he's alone, to fix it. Ed likes to be his own mechanic, and he prides himself on this ability. Today, however, he is tired—didn't get enough sleep last night. First of all, he discovers that he has forgotten to take a necessary tool out of the other car which his family is using today. Now starts the negative mind-feeding: "You Dummy, can't you remember anything?" He then improvises with another tool and accidently drops it into the recesses of the engine. "Butterfingers," he mutters to himself, "You'd think you'd never worked on an engine before." He retrieves the tool and places it where he can get the right amount of leverage and pushes as hard as he can. The tool slips, and he gouges a piece out of his knuckle. "Ouch, what a prize klutz you are! You can't do anything right!" With each piece of inner "downing" dialogue, Ed becomes more impatient with himself and less effective. He isn't able to complete the job before the family returns. The first thing his son says as he jumps out of the car, "How's the car running, Dad? It's in perfect shape, I'll bet!" Ed's negative mind-feeding had to zap him one more time: "You're a fine model for your son—can't even correct a simple engine knock." That puts him on the defensive, and he growls something rude to his son. Those chains of activating events and Ed's berating conversations with himself have put him in a bad mood, and his behaviors are contrary to his usual jovial self. His family is resentful and confused by his behavior, and the rest of the day is rather unpleasant for all of them.

All this might have been avoided if Ed had known about "thought stopping." Thought stopping is Joseph Wolpe's cure for eliminating thoughts that are obsessive and unproductive. The parts of Wolpe's technique which I have found to be most helpful in the area of gaining self-esteem are: (1) *Recognize* that you are indulging in negative mind-feeding. (2) Ask yourself if that kind of talk is really productive for you. (3) **Stop** the counter-productive self talk. (4) Replace it with reassuring or self-accepting statements.

In Ed's case, he would have been aware of his *first* statement to himself, "You Dummy etc." He would surely have seen that this was negative mind-feeding and decided that it would not be productive for him to continue this kind of talk. If he did continue with the negative dialogue when he dropped the wrench, he could say, "**Stop** this severe self talk right now!" He might pause a minute and reflect on how many times he's repaired his motors and the successes he's had in the past. Then, if after replacing the self-accepting statements, he still has trouble; the smart thing for Ed to do would be to leave this task for a period. His thoughts might be, "Guess I'll take a break, I just don't feel like continuing with this right now." Or, "I really didn't sleep well last night, I'm beat—guess I'll rest for a little while and come back to this later." Through this positive thinking—realistic and accurate—Ed has not lost his feeling of self esteem, and he will be able to finish the job more effectively when he returns to it. When we are tired, tense or ill, we are most susceptible to negative mind-feeding. Be especially on the look-out for denigrating your self esteem at those times.

Episode of Jane: Jane came in for counseling. She is a woman who was about to retire from a career in which she had been very successful. She was happy about retiring but felt that her co-workers were perceiving her as "old" and "incapable." She reported that they were taking her off her usual assignments, and everyone seemed to be "patronizing" her. I asked why they were doing this. Her negative explanation was that they undoubtedly found her incompetent, over-the-hill, out-of-it, stodgy, old-fashioned, uninteresting, and that they would be glad to see her go. From those negative thoughts, she began to resent them for these attitudes she felt they had toward her. "After all," she thought, "I helped train most of them. I encouraged them through lots of bad times. I often championed their causes to the people in charge of the office. How ungrateful of them!" And her negative mind-feeding went on and on.

After a few sessions of sharing her feelings, Jane decided that it might be wise to speak with one or two of the group whom she felt closest to and see if her perceptions were accurate. They were not. It seems that the group **had** talked about Jane's retirement, but they all agreed how much they would miss her. They concluded that the nicest thing they could give her—along with the usual farewell dinner—was to make her last months of work as easy and as pleasant as possible. They would handle the "tiresome" jobs and give her the best assignments. They would take time to tell her how great she was and make it a point to invite her out to lunch at least every other week. These were all loving actions which had been interpreted by Jane as demeaning and condescending. Her negative mind-feeding worsened the situation. When Jane found out the facts, her attitude changed remarkably; and her self esteem returned.

This incorporates another phase to add to thought stopping. If your negative mind-feeding persists when you are thinking about another person's actions toward you and what it stems from— **check it out.** There is no way that your mind can give you the reasonable answers. Go to the source of your dilemma—ask the person or persons involved. Nine times out of ten, you are catastrophizing with inaccurate and illogical thoughts. You will often find that their behavior had nothing to do with you, it stemmed from a problem in their life that wasn't remotely related to you.

So, begin today identifying and interrupting irrational or counter-productive thoughts and replacing them with more positive, realistic and useful thoughts. You'll find this will work wonders with your having and keeping self esteem.

If negative mind-feeding has been a pattern of yours—as it has for most of us—be aware that this new attitude takes *practice*; because, it not only involves learning a new skill, but breaking an old habit. So practice, have patience, and be persistent.

It sometimes helps to reward yourself when you succeed at extinguishing these unwanted thoughts. Buy yourself some new clothes, go to a movie you've been wanting to see, or give yourself the luxury to let the dishes go and read that book you've been eyeing. The intrinsic feelings of satisfaction, pride, accomplishment and relief may be reward enough, however. You feel good about yourself; and that's the superlative feeling; one that we all need and search for. Give up the mental conspiracy that negative mind-feeding has against self esteem. You take control of your thoughts; make them the best and most productive for your inner peace and happiness. You can do it!

Your attitude (yours—no one else's) is directly related to whether you have high self esteem or you don't. If your attitude is a positive one, that is: (1) If you recognize and build on your strengths, (2) If you don't demand perfection of yourself and (3) If you replace negative mind-feeding with positive thoughts, you're well on your way to having high self esteem.

Negative Mind-Feeding "Work Outs"

1. When was the most recent time that you engaged in negative mind-feeding?
   (a) What was the activating event?
   (b) What thoughts did you have following that event?
   (c) Check to see how irrational your thinking was.
   (d) How could you have changed your thoughts so that your feelings would improve?

2. Tune into your thoughts. If they are illogical and catastrophizing, say, "**Stop** this negative mind-feeding" and change the subject.

3. When you find that your thoughts are uncomplimentary about yourself, stop immediately and try to replace those derogatory statements with positive ones.
   (a) Remember your strengths and your successes.
   (b) Don't expect perfection.

4. If you persist in replaying a negative tape in your mind, put a rubber band on your wrist and snap it when those thoughts reappear. If you don't have a rubber band, pinch yourself or dig your nails into your palms. That should help extinguish those unwanted thoughts.

5. When you find yourself becoming upset over the actions or reactions of someone, **check it out** as soon as you can. Don't allow yourself to fabricate reasons for their behavior. Hear it from *them*.
   (a) If you can't reach them for a day or two, put it "on hold" until you can speak to them.
   (b) Don't allow yourself to "guess" at why they acted the way they did. That's a sure lead into negative mind-feeding.

6. Stop yourself when you are negative mind-feeding and ask:
   (a) Am I feeling up to par?
   (b) Did I have my usual quota of sleep last night?

(c) Has my routine been upset?

(d) Do I feel things are piling up and closing in on me?

Analyzing the source of the problem often will halt the negative mind-feeding.

> *"Notice the difference between what happens when a man says to himself, "I have failed three times," and what happens when he says, "I am a failure."*
>
> **S.I. Hayakawa**

6

Your Value System

One of the surest ways to get self esteem and keep it is: **live by your value system**. It is when we deviate from the things we believe in that we do harm to our self esteem.

What is a *value system*? First of all, it is *yours*; and it is unique because you are one-of-a-kind. It is your code of ethics by which to live. It is your "behavior-bible." It is what guides your life. Values and actions go hand in hand. It's when they become separated that things go awry. You feel secure, comfortable, satisfied and productive when you are operating according to *your* value system. That brings high self esteem. When your behavior differs from your accepted standards, you lose your self esteem—**fast!**

In order to be certain if your actions are coinciding with your value system, you have to become intimately acquainted with what makes up your value system. At the moment, you are probably consciously or unconsciously aware of *some* of the traits which you value—about you. In order to become familiar with the complete list, I suggest you start by writing down the qualities that you are proud to have. The suggestions that follow may give you a working start, but don't be confined by these. Use your own words or phrases, if you wish—they may feel more comfortable. Add to the following list if there are some qualities you value which have been omitted.

_____ Ambitious (hard-working, aspiring)

_____ Broadminded (open-minded)

_____ Capable (competent, effective)

_____ Cheerful (lighthearted, joyful)

_____ Clean (neat, tidy)

_____ Courageous (standing up for your beliefs)

_____ Forgiving (willing to pardon others)

_____ Helpful (working for the welfare of others)

_____ Honest (sincere, truthful)

_____ Imaginative (daring, creative)

_____ Independent (self-reliant, self-sufficient)

_____ Intellectual (intelligent, reflective)

_____ Logical (consistent, rational)

_____ Loving (affectionate, tender)

_____ Obedient (dutiful, respectful)

_____ Polite (courteous, well-mannered)

_____ Self-controlled (restrained, self-disciplined)

Perhaps you are thinking, "This is difficult, I've spent my life living according to others' values—my parents', my peers', my spouse's, my boss's, family member's, etc. I'm not even sure that I know what *mine* are!"

Hundreds of people with whom I've worked have responded that way. There's a way to remedy that. Check through these traits and challenge each one as to whether it is important to **you.** For instance, "clean (neat, tidy)." "Mmmm I really don't care that much if my room is neat or not, but mother was so insistent that it be 'just so' that even now I feel guilty if something is out of place."

If this isn't a trait that *you* value, don't put it down as part of your value system. Stop being shackled by the restraints of parents', peers', spouse's or family's value systems. Free yourself by establishing your own. You will choose *some* of the qualities which others have espoused, but claim them now as yours—not theirs....Give yourself the power to make these decisions; you're the one who has to live by them. You can't have high self esteem unless you are living by your own value system.

Take a look at each quality and ask yourself, "Is it important to me that I behave in this manner?" If it is, put it on your list: it is then **your** choice. If, when you ask that question, the answer is negative, then cross it off; it doesn't belong on your list. When you have examined and reviewed each item carefully and have either claimed it for your own or disposed of it, you have the beginning of your value system.

When you have completed your list of prized qualities, check the ten which you value most. Take a good look at them; they are the nucleus of **your** value system. As with your attitude, **you** are in charge of your value system. Put this list where you can refer to it often. Add to it when another attribute appears which you revere in yourself. Also, alter your value system occasionally when you find that there is a change in priority of the items. Our values *do* change throughout our lives.

All right, I assume that you have masterminded the authoring of your value system. Now, let's proceed to gaining the understanding of how living by this system can affect your self esteem. Think of a time when you felt "down" on yourself—unworthy— a real "nothing"! What were your actions preceding these feelings of low self esteem? Chances are, they were actions which were diametrically opposed to **your value system!** For instance: if one of your top 10 values is "kindness", and you had said some terribly unkind things to a friend, you clearly felt miserable, guilty, uncomfortable and ashamed. Your self esteem was at low tide. **You** were responsible for making yourself feel so wretched. You acted against your value system. That's the quickest way to lose self esteem. "To thine own self be true" still makes a lot of sense.

Here are some examples of instances when people did not live by their rules of behavior.

"Being a good Christian is part of my value system. A few years ago I was so unsure of myself that I was embarrassed to say grace in a restaurant. I felt so guilty that I could not enjoy my meal. I was not living by my own standards."

"One of the things that I value most about myself is my honesty. Recently, I prepared my income tax and neglected to include some interest payments which I receive every month. It seemed more advantageous to me at the time to just skip those items. As the result of my dishonesty, I became anxious, got knots in my stomach and was disappointed in myself. These feelings of discomfort brought me around to realizing I had been dishonest, and I did not like me. I called the accountant and instructed him to add the interest figures which I had excluded. My anxiety was reduced, and I felt much better about myself."

"One of my values is my physical health. When I don't do my exercises on a daily basis and watch my diet, I feel upset and am very unhappy with myself."

"The parts of my value system that are included in this example are "self-control" and "forgiveness." Recently, I had an unfortunate run-in with my neighbor. After the episode, I felt angry at myself, because I was not as *self-controlled* as I might have been. I analyzed it all; and, although I feel she was mostly at fault, for my peace of mind I must *forgive* her. I will do my part toward a reconciliation, because I have felt bad about myself ever since."

So much for the "bad news," now look at the other side of the coin—how to have high self esteem. You act in harmony with your value system. Haven't you at times felt at peace with yourself—contented, fulfilled and happy? No, I'm not talking about the feeling after a sumptuous meal or a "close encounter" with that special someone. I'm referring to that feeling that comes after you did something that made you feel proud of yourself—something which corresponded to your value system. Take note of the times you have these marvelous feelings and trace it back to the source: your actions which preceded the feelings. These actions were ones which you value. Make this game of searching for the link between your behaviors and your feelings of accomplishment a habit. You may find a new value to add to your list.

Living by one's value system **works**; it brings high self esteem. Here are some examples:

"A value I cherish is my broadmindedness. Recently, someone very dear to me started living with her boy friend. This went against my code of proper behavior; but, since it fit into their lifestyle, it was none of my business. I continued to love them as before. I felt good knowing that I had been broadminded."

"A value I have is my spiritual development. Whenever I meditate and pray and read spiritual affirmations, I feel centered and able to flow with life in a loving and happy way."

"Honesty is on my value system. When I act completely honest, I feel happy and undisturbed. An example of this was when I was dining out and the waitress forgot to include a charge for a salad I ordered a la carte. I could have easily let it go as her mistake and paid the lesser amount. Instead, I called her to my table and pointed out her error. She promptly corrected the bill and thanked me for calling it to her attention. That gave me a satisfied feeling."

"I pride myself on being "friendly." At lunch one day I met an elderly couple from out of town. They seemed lost; so I said they could join me, and I would help them find their way around. They were delightful! They were so appreciative, and we talked and had a great time. I enjoyed the afternoon and feel I have new friends. We plan to see each other again. Because of living by my value, I feel almost 'high'."

Now that you realize the importance of living by your value system, I hope you have your current list intact, temporarily. Keep it handy for easy reference and continue to monitor your actions to discover new values which you can add to your list.

Living in accordance with your value system is good for your self esteem. It is important to be cognizant of each value and its priority. For, living with an "outdated" value system can be *harmful* to your self esteem.

"Outdated" value systems occur when (1) values change in priority, and (2) when values become impossible to hold on to.

(1) Our values do change in importance; some by choice and some by circumstances.

You can note a change in priority by paying close attention to your actions. A change in your behavior will reflect a change in priority.

Example of change in priority. Kevin was a freshman in college. High on his value system was "being an intellectual"; he prided himself on his good study habits and good grades.

Through a friend, Kevin became interested in becoming a fireman. The requirements of the fire department for physical strength were stringent. Kevin was out of shape. He had spent much more time studying than exercising. Now, however, "physical conditioning" became higher and more important on his value system. "Being an intellectual" dropped in precedence at this time. Kevin noted this and adjusted his list. He changed the position of these two qualities. This was his choice and he was comfortable with it. He did not continue to "hit the books" as if this were still his highest ranked value, but acted on his new-number-one-value—"physical conditioning." This was a changing of priorities by *his* choosing. He had charge of his value system.

Another example. Norma had been a fastidious person all her life. She valued her appearance; and, for years, "an attractive appearance" was topmost on her value system list. "Sociability" was also one of her top values. She liked to hobnob with her fellow workers at lunch.

Norma was a workaholic and began to realize that she needed more exercise to keep herself physically fit and mentally relaxed. But when was there time to exercise?

A block from where Norma worked was a park. She had an hour for lunch every day which she used for socializing. If she went to the park and walked briskly for half an hour, she would have to forego lunch with the "gang." Besides that, she could get rained on, windblown and sweaty! She perhaps would not look as well groomed when she returned to work.

Norma chose to put "health" at the top of her value system—placing "sociability" and "an attractive appearance" in secondary positions. *She* was in charge; *she* made the decisions; *she* changed her list; she was happy!

Sometimes circumstances direct us to make a change in our value systems.

For example: Susan was married—a mother of three children —and she worked hard to be "a good wife and mother." This was at the pinnacle of her value system.

But after fifteen years of marriage, she and her husband got a divorce. Now she found it necessary to look for a job to support herself and her children. Because of a change in her life's pattern, "earning a living" suddenly became number one on her value system. "Being a good wife" was scratched off the list; and "being a good mother" became part of "earning a living."

Susan adjusted her value system to match her activities of the present.

So, you see, rank and position for items on your value system do change. With that in mind, you should check this out periodically.

Then, (2) there are the values which become impossible to keep on your list. If we maintain their presence on our value system, we are miserable, pining for the past, and our self esteem suffers.

Examples of these "extinct" values are:

Joe attended high school in a small town. He was active in football, basketball, and baseball. He played on the first team in each of these sports. "Being an outstanding athlete in team sports" was first on his value system list. He gained much of his self esteem through his outstanding participation in athletics.

Joe graduated from high school and went on to a major university. Naturally, he tried out for the team in each of the three sports he had excelled in in high school. He was not chosen to be a member of any of the teams! This was a blow to his self esteem. He felt confused and unsure of himself until he replaced "being an outstanding athlete in team sports" with "studying to be a coach." He didn't allow his self esteem to evaporate; he changed his value system and went on with his life. He replaced an "impossible" value with a realistic one.

Another example:

Ann had a beautiful singing voice; she enjoyed this talent and valued it in herself. She was much in demand to sing at special events; her solos were sought after throughout the community. She was proud of this.

Over the years, her voice began to lose its resonance; she didn't feel as sure of herself when she performed. Others were asked to sing where she had once been the "star." She practiced less often; and, when she did, she realized that she didn't have the power and control over her voice that she had in the past. This made her discouraged and sad; she fretted over this loss, and her self esteem dissolved.

Ann was so upset that she sought professional help to restore her self esteem. She learned to find new, realistic values to rebuild her self esteem. She joined the church choir and enjoyed singing with the other members; she was content to let others do the solos.

She also enjoyed the comradeship that working in the choir and in the church circle gave her. "Being a team member in the church" replaced the value of "having a lovely singing voice." She was happy being one of the group as opposed to being the "star." Sometimes being the star had been lonely; and, just a year ago, Ann's husband had died. She felt herself needing to reach out and make new friends. Her values changed with changes in her life. Ann felt good about making these changes and is now leading a happy, productive life.

So be alert to changes in rank order of your values *and* those that need to be removed. We cannot cash in on *past* values; our self esteem won't buy that. If we hold on to outmoded values as the reference for our self esteem or grieve over their loss, *we* are destroying our self worth.

You are in charge of changing your value system. There are two ways in which you can adjust to a value which becomes outdated: (1) Eliminate it completely and replace it with a new value as Joe did, **or** (2) transfer it to your "**memory value system.**"

By transferring it to your "**memory value system**," you don't blot out the old value completely; but, rather, you place it where you can view it from a healthy perspective. You can reflect, with joy, on the values you cherished. You look at the "**memory value system**" with pride and satisfaction in remembering past experiences and feelings—instead of feeling empty by their disappearance from your current value system. Or, you can leave them on your current value system and remind yourself daily that they are impossible values by which you measure your worth. Make the transfer *today!*

It is my belief that we all have values that could be placed on our memory list. Let extinct values disappear or take their rightful place on your "**memory value system**"—to be recalled with nostalgic joy.

Beverly Sills is a good model for this behavior. She says, "When I retired from singing to take on my present job, I made a total break. I won't even hum in the shower. My voice had a nonstop career for more than thirty-five years, and it deserves to be put to bed with dignity, not yanked out every once in a while to see if it can still do what it used to do. It can't."

You can see that living by your updated value system is crucial to your having high self esteem. We will discuss in another chapter how being familiar with your value system is also necessary for retrieving self esteem when it leaves for a period.

So, make it a point to write down your value system, check on it often for accuracy and timeliness; and, then, **live by it!**

Your Value System "Work Outs"

Have your list of values handy when you do these work outs.
1. Check over your current **value system** list.

   (a) Are there values on this list that you're still carrying around with you from the past that were someone else's values?

   (b) If so, scrutinize them and determine whether you wish to keep them as **yours.**

   (c) If not, scratch them off and eliminate them from your list.

   (d) If you wish to keep them, leave them on the list and label them as *your* values.

2. Think of a time recently when you felt "down" on yourself (through some action of your own).

   (a) Check your value system to see which value or values you violated.

   (b) Perhaps you have neglected to put this value on the list. If so, add it **now.**

3. Think of a time recently when you felt satisfied or excited about yourself.

   (a) Check your value system and note which value or values you were acting out.

   (b) If you don't have the value on your list that was responsible for your approving feeling of yourself, add it.

4. Check your value system list for changes in priority.

   (a) If you discovered some changes, what caused the change?

   (b) Be sure that you alter your list to reflect these changes.

5. Are there any values on your list that should be eliminated or transferred to your **memory value system?**

   (a) If you have begun your **memory value system**, and you wish to transfer a value from your current value system, do it **now.**

6. Look over your **memory value system.**

   (a) Think carefully about each item on this list.

(b) Does thinking about these "past" values make you happy or sad?

    1. If it makes you sad, you are still holding on to them as if they were possible; that's not good for your self esteem.

    2. If remembering this value makes you happy, it's in the right place, and you have cut the umbilical cord from the current value system. Good for you!

"No man is an island entire of itself; every man is a piece of the continent, a part of the main..."

John Donne

7

Your Support System

As I have said in previous chapters, it is neither wise nor healthy to depend exclusively on others for our self esteem. That leaves too much to the whims of others—which is out of our control. We are dependent, however, in part on other people's appraisals for our self confidence. As I write, I have a letter from my father which says, "Didn't know you were writing a book on your favorite subject. Good luck, I know you can do it!" Many times during these months, I have looked at that letter and been encouraged to continue.

Maslow's hierarchy for self actualization places "love and belongingness" and "esteem by others" as **basic needs**. One of his three major antecedents of self esteem is "respect and approval from other people."

Another giant in the field of psychology, Carl Rogers, concludes that part of the scheme for a fully-functioning person is—"the individual has a need for positive regard."

Karen Horney concurs with this statement when she emphasizes, "a healthy personality must have the feeling of being competent and *lovable*."

These statements have proved to be true—time after time— in my counseling with people on self esteem. One former drug addict shared with me that he had given up on himself, but his parents "hung in there" and helped renew his faith in himself so that he sought counseling and kicked the habit.

Another counselee explained that she never would have made it through the nursing program without the support, love, understanding, and encouragement of a close friend.

We need that special validation and affirmation of our worth. Each of us looks for the warmth of others' respect and approval. We thrive on the nourishment of positive regard from others.

Eric Berne suggests that "strokes" from others are as necessary to human life as are any of the other primary biological needs—such as the need for food, water, and shelter. What Berne pointed out has been researched in recent studies of longevity. Scientists have found that people live longer and happier lives if they have a close cohort with whom they share their thoughts and experiences.

This all leads to the next step in building self esteem. Again, it is something over which you have control—**your support system**. By support system, I refer to the people who are the source of **your** validation and appreciation.

I have separated these people into four different groups: (1) the close support group, (2) the non-contributing group, (3) the destructive group, and (4) the prospective friends group.

By carefully examining your present support system, you may find you will choose to make some changes in order to enhance your self esteem. Remember, every positive and affirming behavior by another to you is a stimulus to raising your self esteem. Therefore, the quality of your support system is vital to your positive self image.

Look at each group and determine how it relates to your support system. Don't forget, it's **your** support system—you have control over it!

First there is the **close support group**. These are the special people who are supportive, understanding, loving, patient, helpful, interested, and sensitive to your needs and wishes. I have a plaque which hangs in my office which describes this group well. It's entitled "Friendship," and it was written by Dinah Maria Mulcok Criak. "Oh the comfort, the inexpressible comfort of feeling safe with a person, having neither to weigh thoughts nor measure words but to pour them all right out, just as they are, chaff and grain together knowing that a faithful hand will take

SUPPORT SYSTEM

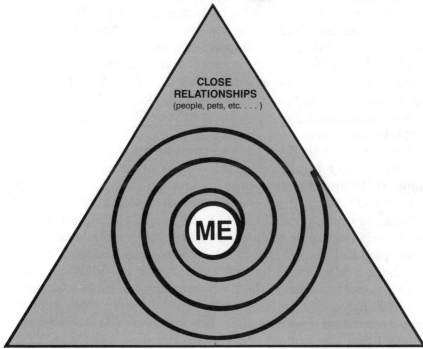

PROSPECTIVE FRIENDS

CLOSE
RELATIONSHIPS
(people, pets, etc. . . .)

ME

NON CONTRIBUTING
RELATIONSHIPS

DESTRUCTIVE
RELATIONSHIPS
(critical, possessive, domineering)

Diagram 3

and sift them, keep what is worth keeping, and then, with a breath of kindness, blow the rest away."

The Close Support Group are the priceless people in our lives who help us realize the meaning of our existence. They know the "real" you; they understand where we've been; and they help us to grow.

As you will note in the diagram, I include pets in this group. Many people receive important love messages from their pets that makes them feel needed and important. These are feelings which promote the growth of self esteem.

I spoke with a woman who had recently been widowed. She said that her only contact for weeks after her husband's death was their faithful dog. The dependence and adoration of this pet enabled her to make it through an almost unbearable period. Once through that time of grief, she was able to face the world again and soon was back socializing with their circle of friends.

So, if you have a pet who belongs in your Close Support Group, add it to the others.

We are fortunate if we have as many as three or four individuals who really fulfill the qualifications of being in the Close Support Group. We are doubly fortunate if they live near us. In this mobile society where people are changing jobs and residences often, it's difficult to keep your Close Support Group near you. Geographic distance, however, cannot dilute the closeness you feel for each other. I have Close Support Group members in Montana, Minnesota, Nebraska and Idaho. A letter or phone call from one of them will boost my self esteem for days.

Write down the persons and/or pets in **your close support group** and count your blessings! It is most essential for your self concept that you protect and nourish these relationships. They, in essence, **are** your primary support system. Too often we take these individuals for granted. Of all the groups in your support system, this is the group which deserves the largest share of your time and energy and love. They deserve the best you have to give!

The awareness to have about these special people is: **Take care of each and every one of them. Without them, your outside needs for unconditional positive regard will not be met.** They are perhaps more consistently loving of you than you are of yourself. These are the people to be cherished in your life. Do something about that **today!** Share your loving thoughts with them by phone, letter or face to face.

The second group in your support system is made up of **non-contributing relationships**. Do you have any friends like that? They are the people whom you may see quite often; they're O.K.—pleasant, fun to be with; but they don't contribute much to your positive self concept. They are more concerned with "telling" you, rather than listening to you; they are happy to take from you; but they don't often reciprocate. They aren't the ones whom you'd call on if you really needed help. These are the "innocuous individuals" as far as helping to develop your self esteem.

The awareness to have about this group is: **they are a "neutral" group. They don't affect your self esteem much — either way.**

It's up to you to decide how much time and energy you want to spend with this group.

The destructive group needs your close scrutiny and consideration for they are the "killers" of self esteem! They are the friends or family who show their "caring" through being overly critical, overly protective, domineering, jealous, perpetually pessimistic, demandingly dogmatic or possessive. None of these attitudes and behaviors help foster self-love.

It's often shocking and baffling how much time we spend with these destructive relationships. It's as if we were locked into them and are unable to find the key to release us.

The key is to be aware that: **these people are damaging to your self esteem every time you are with them.** Therefore, it might be wise to be with them as seldom as possible.

Sometimes that is difficult; they may be part of your family, and circumstances force you to be with them often. In that case, you have several alternatives: (1) cut down on the amount of time you spend with them; (2) spend the same amount of time with them but try to ignore—or become immune—to their destructive influences; (3) spend no time with them at all; or (4) confront them with the problem—talk it over. It could be that they are unaware of their destructive behavior. Or, if they are aware of it, it may be worth it to them to change if they think that persisting in this behavior will sacrifice your relationship.

Whatever your choice, you **do** have options in dealing with these people. You merely have to make the choice that will be most comfortable and appropriate for you.

Let's say tht your choice might be to go on exposing yourself to this punishment (this is **not** the choice that I would suggest unless

you can block out their behaviors which are destructive to you).
However, if this is your choice, then realize that **you** are responsible for subjecting yourself to this treatment, **and** you are also
responsible for reinforcing this person's negative behavior. This
is not healthy for either of you. You are allowing them to "chip
away" at your self esteem; and you are also protecting them
from the natural consequences of their behavior. Hence, they
have little motivation or reason to change. Do you want to be
responsible for that?

If it's happiness, peace, pride in yourself, and productivity you
want, **do** something about your relating to the people in your
Destructive Group.

Here's an example of how George handled this problem.

George was feeling low; he was forever trying to keep up with
his old school buddy. When they were on the high school basketball team, Arnie was always the star; Arnie made the baskets;
George fed him the ball.

When they went to college, they both took business as their
major. George had to work his way through school, so his grades
were not as high as Arnie's. Arnie would make remarks like:
"Good old George, you try so hard; but you never make A's like I
do; it seems easy for me to make A's!"

After college, they each worked for the same big corporation.
Arnie advanced rapidly; George was right behind him.

They belonged to the same social clubs, and their families
were together for holidays. Always, Arnie was the leader, the
teller-of-stories, the one who tooted his own horn. George was
often the butt of his jokes.

George's close support group—his wife and children—tried
to suggest that maybe Arnie wasn't contributing to George's
success or happiness. George would reply, "Oh, he doesn't mean
anything by that insulting talk; he's been a friend for a long
time."

There were other men in the company who asked George to
play golf on weekends or invited him for poker parties. Often
George declined the invitations or asked if Arnie could be
included.

George's self esteem got lower and lower. He went for
counseling. In getting in touch with his true feelings, George was
able to see that Arnie was a destructive friend.

He decided to spend more time and energy with his immediate

support system; he had often neglected them to do things with Arnie. He also began to accept invitations to enjoy activities with new friends. He soon realized that he was happier and felt better about himself when he wasn't around Arnie so much. His self esteem was strengthened by being with other people.

The last group of people who may be just entering your support system are the **prospective friends group.** They are the persons "out there" whom you've singled out as wanting to know better. Throughout our lives, we gather in new friends by seeking out and getting to know individuals from the Prospective Friends Group.

The awareness which is significant to have about this group is: **these "unknowns" may eventually fit into one of the other three groups in your support system.** Hopefully, they will become a member of the valued Close Support Group. Some of your present Close Support Group undoubtedly were prospective friends at one time. It takes time for someone to truly meet the requirements for this coveted group.

Prospective friends may also be candidates for the Destructive and the Non-Contributing Groups. Be on the lookout for actions and words that may place them in one or the other of these.

Sometimes something within us, a need or compulsion, makes us choose as friends people who have the same destructive qualities from which we are trying to disengage ourselves. Beware of this.

A young woman habitually came to see me when she had a "crisis" with her male-companion-of-the-moment. After seeing her sporadically over a two year period, I noted a distinct pattern to her problems. She was inclined to become involved with men who could not, or would not satisfy her needs. The beginning of their relationship was always "perfect"; soon it would deteriorate into constant arguing and then escalate into a hurtful parting.

After three of these shattering experiences, Jan decided to come for counseling once a week. During these sessions she realized that she was choosing men whom she could "rescue." One had been an alcoholic, one an ex-convict, and one couldn't hold down a job. She also saw that, in each relationship, she began to resent always having to give to them; she wanted her needs fulfilled, too. By that stage in the relationship, each man was taking more and more—both materially and psychologically from her and resisted her changing her original "selfless" role. Each man became angry and confused when she demanded that he do "this or that" for her. And so, each relationship ended unhappily.

Jan recognized that she often chose people in her Prospective Friends Group who had the same qualities of those in her Destructive Relationships Group. She vowed to change this.

When she would meet a new man, she carefully observed whether he would be one who could satisfy her needs — rather than having to be rescued. That was the way to find a close, long-term, satisfying relationship which she so wanted.

Jan took charge of her support system, and it made an appreciable difference in her life. She regained her self respect.

Often, we have **secondary** support systems which give us additional support in specific areas of our lives.

Your **secondary** support system could be any one of the following: a **Work** Support System, an **Organizational** Support System, a **Church** Support System, a **Neighborhood** Support System, a **Country Club** Support System, a **School** Support System, etc.

The classifications of the four different groups within these **secondary** support systems are the same as for your **primary** support system. The Close Support Group is to be appreciated; the Non-Contributing Group is to be seen as just that; the Destructive Group is to be viewed as the group that destroys your self esteem; and the Prospective Friends Group may have members who will enter the other three groups.

These **secondary** support systems are valuable in raising your self esteem. Not *as* valuable as the **primary** support system, but still important to your having feelings of self satisfaction in these different parts of your life.

For instance, on your job, there might be a person in your **Work** Support System who is important to you and is a member of that system's Close Support Group. This person praises your efforts on the job, encourages you in each new undertaking, and is always there when you need assistance. Every day, when you go to work, you look forward to seeing this friend. It could be that you never see him or her during your "off-work" hours. Even so, they are an important anchor to your feeling relaxed, productive, and appreciated at work. This is meaningful to keeping your self esteem high, since we often spend a large proportion of our waking hours at work.

Or, in your **Neighborhood** Support System, there may be that special individual whom you don't see often, but you know is always there. When you are together, you get a "lift" from this person's complimentary comments and caring concern about you. If there is ever anything you need—from a cup of sugar to a ride to the store—this is whom you call on and are never disappointed. You undoubtedly consider this person as one of your Close Support Group in your **Neighborhood** Support System. He or she is a great help in your having high self esteem.

We have dealt with the **Secondary** support systems only superficially. It is interesting at times to look at these sub-groups and see how they affect your life. Your main focus, however, should be with your **primary** support system; that's the one we are referring to when we talk about "your support system." This is the one that is the foundation for your self esteem.

As you become more perceptive and discriminating about your support system, you will find your self esteem improving and strengthening. As a consequence of feeling good about yourself, you will be more expressive, self-enhancing, and honest in your relationships. As a result of these behaviors, more people will be attracted to you and want to be with you. You will gain more respect from others. Your support system will grow. It's the old *positive* self esteem cycle working again. (See Diagram One.)

Your support system can be one of the strongest allies to your self esteem; or it can attack and weaken it. It's all up to **you!**

Your Support System "Work Outs"

1. Make a list of those in your Close Support Group.

    (a) Are your time and energy going to these individuals?

    (b) Are you letting them know that they *are* your Close Support Group?

    (c) If the answers to the above questions are, "no," you are not taking care of the special someones who nurture your self esteem.

        1. Do something loving for them **today**!

2. Who are the persons in your Non-Contributing Group?

    (a) Are you aware that the time and energy you spend with these people keeps your self esteem at *status quo*?

3. Take a good look at each person in your Destructive Relationships Group.

    (a) What do you plan to do in each situation?

    (b) Are you willing to sacrifice your self esteem by not changing these relationships or your attitude toward them?

4. Is there a person or two in your Prospective Friends Group at the moment?

    (a) What are you doing to get better acquainted with them?

    (b) Are they candidates for any of the other groups in your support system?

    (c) Are you on the look-out for destructive behaviors and attitudes in these people?

        1. If you have spotted some destructive qualities, are you still pursuing the relationship?

5. If you have a job or career, note how the people where you work fit into each of the groups in your **Work** Support System.

    (a) Are you dealing with the people in each group so that it will be constructive to your self esteem?

6. Do you have any other **Secondary** support systems?

    (a) Write down the names of the people who fit into each of the four groups in that particular support system.

    (b) Think of things that could be done with these individuals to improve your self esteem.

"What would life be if we had no courage to attempt anything?"

Vincent van Gogh

Goal-Setting

(Seven Steps to Self Esteem)

You are now familiar with most of the skills you need for acquiring high self esteem.

First, developing a positive attitude by: looking at your strengths, by not expecting to be perfect, and by stopping your negative mind-feeding.

Next, you have developed your value system and have practiced living according to it.

Then, you have checked your support system and have taken the necessary steps to making it compatible with having high self esteem.

Now, you are ready for the final skill—**Goal-Setting.**

A goal is a purpose toward which your effort is directed. We all feel better about ourselves if we feel our life has purpose. What is important is not so much the kind of goal one sets, but its achievement. Accomplishment of a personal goal—whether it be in a physical, intellectual, or social realm, can be a self-enhancing experience. If you feel that you have reached the goals you set up for yourself, you probably have high self esteem. If you feel that you have failed in your attempt to reach these goals, you are likely to have low self esteem.

There is a direct relationship between goal achievement and

high self esteem. **You** are in charge of setting and reaching your goals. It is all under your control!

There are certain, specific steps to follow when setting up your goals so that the results will be positive; and high self esteem will be the result. If you don't rigidly adhere to these guidelines, it could lead to disappointment in not reaching your goals.

Step 1.   **Start out by setting a short term goal so that you will feel the thrill of success right away!** For instance, if you have been trying to get a start on figuring your income tax; set a goal of getting all your receipts gathered together by the weekend coming up. That's short term. The accomplishment of a short term goal will make you feel good about yourself. Or, you may want to view "mini goals" leading to a long term goal as short term goals. The longer term goal would be: to send in your income tax March 1st. You may wish to set this goal up in January. The short term goals or mini goals leading up to the completion of the long term goal would be:

a) get papers gathered and in order by   Jan. 30

b) review last year's income tax forms by   Feb. 15

c) do computing and make rough draft of
        copies by   Feb. 25

d) prepare final copies by   Feb. 28

e) send in completed forms by   March 1

Each of the auxiliary steps to the long term goal can be classified as short term goals or mini goals. Some people work better with one short term goal at a time. Others prefer to have mini goals which lead to the ultimate larger goal. Both approaches bring a feeling of accomplishment; and, therefore, enhance self esteem.

Step 2.   **Be absolutely certain that the goal you set up is** *your* **goal; something** *you* **desire to achieve.** If it isn't, chances are you won't be seriously motivated to follow through and complete the goal.

Wrong Way: Dorothy was a poor bridge player; she wasn't much interested in bridge. Her husband urged her to take lessons at the local community college so that she would improve her bidding and her playing. Dorothy reluctantly signed up for a non-credit course and attended about half of the classes. She didn't achieve the goal of improving her bridge playing, because it wasn't **her** goal, but she felt bad about herself for quitting.

Right Way: Jerry wanted to learn to shoot skeet. He had the proper equipment but not the money to pay for the expenses of trapshooting. So, he got a job and worked a forty hour week — besides going to school — so that he could make enough to take lessons and enjoy the sport. It was not easy; in order to get his studying done, he had to shorten his hours of sleep. He was so busy with work and studying that he cut down drastically on his social life. But, it all seemed worth it to Jerry. He did learn to shoot skeet and has become quite proficient at the sport. He attends the "shoots" and has won several ribbons. Jerry felt wonderful about accomplishing his goal. He worked hard to learn the skill, because it was **his goal!**

Step 3. **Be sure that your goal is attainable — not too easy — but not too difficult.** If it is not attainable, you are setting yourself up for failure. This is destructive to your self esteem. If the goal is not somewhat challenging, you will belittle your success in reaching it. This is no boost to your self image.

Wrong Way: Mike is one of the pitchers on the varsity baseball team. Just last month, the coach had agreed to let him change positions — from short stop to pitcher. Mike was thrilled; he had always wanted to pitch on the varsity team as he had been the pitcher for his high school team.

His *unrealistic* goal was: to be one of the top two pitchers on the varsity team by the end of the season. Mike had tough competition; the other pitchers had two year's experience on the team. Mike was just a freshman.

He sat on the bench most of the season; he was crushed. He blamed himself; he blamed the coach; he blamed his teammates; he blamed his girl friend. The trouble wasn't with any of those people—including himself. The trouble was that his goal was unrealistic; it was an unattainable goal within that time frame and with those circumstances. Mike felt that he wasn't worth much. This stemmed from setting up a goal which was too difficult.

Right Way: Mary wanted to lose 5 pounds in 6 weeks. It was difficult for her to diet—but not impossible. She had lost weight in the past and knew that this was possible to lose 5 pounds in this length of time. Mary marked the calendar when she started and the date by which she hoped to lose the 5 pounds. She put herself on a routine of diet and exercise. It wasn't easy, but she stuck to it. By the end of six weeks, she had lost 7 pounds. Mary felt proud of herself; she looked better; she felt better physically; and her self esteem was high. Her goal had been attainable.

Step 4. **Your goal should be measureable—in time, quality, or quantity.** In order to experience self-approval, set your goal up so that it can be measured. That way, you will know for sure that you have been successful, and that's good for self esteem.

Wrong Way: Julie announced to her friends, more than once, "Sometime I'm going to improve my typing." These were very non-specific terms. "Sometime" could mean a week, a year, five years, etc. Julie did try, periodically, to concentrate on improving her speed and accuracy. She typed her letters—instead of writing them in long hand. Occasionally, when the spirit moved her, she would sit down for an hour and bang away on her typewriter. When friends asked her how she was getting along with improving her typing, she'd reflect, "Oh, I've been working at it some; but I still make lots of errors, and I don't know if my speed has improved or not. Guess

I'll just always be a lousy typist." Not the most encouraging answer for her self esteem. She had no way to measure her improvement. She didn't time her speed when she started—or count her errors. Therefore, she had no way to measure her improvement.

Not having a certain time frame was a deterrent, too, since she didn't have any guidelines within which to operate.

Clearly, this was an unmeasurable goal because of her neglect in tabulating the beginning data to have for comparison *whenever* she terminated her effort to "improve" her typing. This left Julie feeling defeated.

Right Way: Mary set up a goal to make a quilt for her daughter's bed by December 1st; it was to be a Christmas gift. She set up mini goals that led to her completing the finished product. (a) Purchase material and pattern, (b) embroider 12 squares, (c) piece squares together, (d) tuft three layers, (e) finish edges. Each of these goals was measurable, and Mary felt accomplished after finishing each one. She gave her daughter the quilt for Christmas and felt most pleased with herself. Reaching the goal was measured by its completion. Mary's self esteem soared!

Step 5.   **Write the goal down; or tell somebody.**

We take ourselves more seriously when we commit ourselves by "documenting" our intentions. One caution, however, if you do decide to *tell* someone, be sure that it's someone who won't sarcastically "dig" at you if you shouldn't reach your goal. Tell only the *most supportive* of your friends and family. Many people prefer to just write it down— a pledge to themselves concerning this goal.

Wrong Way: Betty noticed a mole on her leg which was turning dark and seemed to be sore. Sometimes it bled. Betty was terrified. She kept telling herself that she should make an appointment with a doctor to have it examined. But, she kept putting it off because of what the diagnosis might be. She just went on worrying—taking no action. This made her feel angry with herself, and her self esteem dwindled.

Right Way: In this same situation, Betty turned to her best friend. She shared her concern and her reluctance to make the doctor's appointment. In talking with her friend, she promised that she would call the doctor the next day and set up an appointment as soon as the doctor could see her. She had made a commitment—both to herself *and* to her close friend. With these factors as motivators, Betty called and made the appointment. She felt satisfied with herself that she had finally made the call.

Step 6. **Your goal should be under your control — as much as possible.** If reaching your goal depends on the weather or requires the involvement of others, there are too many chances that something might go wrong that was not related at all to your efforts.

Wrong Way: John was excited; his goal was to give the family a super summer vacation by flying them all to Hawaii for two weeks! He enjoyed making all the arrangements and thinking how happy and surprised they'd all be. Surprised, yes; happy, **no!** It seemed that his son had already accepted a job as life guard at the pool for the summer; his daughter wanted to travel by car to the Northwest with a group of her friends; his wife was involved in a golf tournament and had a good chance of winning the first flight. They didn't go to Hawaii. John was angry and disappointed; he felt unappreciated and deflated. His plan to give the family a surprise vacation was dependent on too many others who had their own goals for the summer. It was out of his control.

Right Way: Janet's goal was to start art lessons during her summer vacation. She knew of an artist whom she admired who had just announced that she would be offering a series of instructions in the neighboring city. Janet had the time, the money, the transportation, the necessary supplies. She called as soon as she saw the announcement and reserved a space for the series. She felt excited and happy with herself for arranging something she had wanted to do for a long time. Her goal was under her control.

Step 7.   **Set up only** *one* **goal at a time.** If you set up more than one goal at a time, you fall into the "New Year's Resolutions Trap." That's when you resolve to start the new year by cutting down on your drinking, give up smoking, go to bed each night at a reasonable hour, don't waste so much time watching T.V., etc. Your energies and concentration are split among *all* these goals. This leads to frustration and, eventually, to giving up the whole package; and then feeling guilty and disappointed in yourself. If your goal is to give up smoking **or** give up drinking; you usually give up, **period!** So, set *one* goal and strive for that.

Wrong Way: Bill set out to make some changes in his life. He was overweight, smoked too much, didn't exercise and worked nights and weekends at his job. All in all, he was in poor shape. His goals were to eat less, smoke less, drink less, exercise more, and spend more time with his family. It was difficult to cut down on his calories since he had to do business over lunch at a restaurant. How can you concentrate on the business deal when you're counting calories? So, he decided that cutting down on his smoking would be easier. It wasn't. You *have* to smoke after a meal. And so on. He then tried to put himself on a schedule to exercise. When? No time. If he took time to exercise, he'd have to spend more time at the office than he did now. So, that was out! He'd try to cut down on working extra hours so he could spend more time with his family. But how was that possible? They were just making ends meet now. If he worked any less, they'd be in debt. Bill ended up frustrated and angry at himself for not being able to do any of the things he wanted

to do. His thoughts and efforts were fragmented
with too many goals at one time. If you have more
than one goal at a time, it is too tempting to drop
one when the going gets tough and hop on to the
other goal or goals.

Right Way: Ruth was a woman in her thirties. She never had
been able to let her fingernails grow to an attractive length. Her goal was to have longer nails in
six weeks—long enough to have a manicure! She
set up this goal in a self esteem class and announced to the other members of the group what
she intended to accomplish by the end of the semester. At the end of that period, the members of the
class checked on each others' goal achievements.
Sure enough, there was Ruth, wearing a big smile
and holding up her freshly manicured nails for all
to see! She felt terribly proud of herself. She had
done something she had wanted to do for years.
Now, she could go on and set up another objective
to pursue.

Reaching goals is a way of getting high self esteem. The
method of reaching your goals is by following "The 7 Steps of
Goal-Setting." The omission of any one of the steps can be a
deterrent to your reaching your goal. Make it a practice when
you are setting up a new goal to check conscientiously to see that
you: (1) set a short term goal or have mini goals which lead to a
long term goal; (2) are certain that it is **your** goal; (3) are sure that
your goal is challenging but achievable; (4) that it is measurable; (5) that you write it down and/or tell an appropriate loved
one; (6) that it is, as much as possible, under your control; and (7)
that you set up only one goal at a time.

Soon these steps will become second nature and you will reap
the rewards of accomplishing more of your objectives. That, in
turn, will be a producer of self esteem.

If, occasionally, you find that your goal is inappropriate, unnecessary, or was the result of bad judgement at the time you set
it up—recognize this and drop it. You are in charge. You can
stop at any time and drop it for a new one. Allow yourself that
flexibility. Pursuing a poor goal will not give your self esteem a
lift.

Then, there are times, when even though you follow each of the seven steps—to the letter, something comes up to prevent you from reaching the goal. Do you whip yourself and begin some negative mind-feeding? That's not contributive to having high self esteem. We all fail at times; nobody's perfect. The thing to do when this happens, is to ferret out the reasons—realize it wasn't your fault. Or, if you *were* in error, learn by your mistake.

Here's a quote from a woman who set her goal to finish four paintings by the end of the school year. "I finished two paintings. That wasn't my goal, but I realize that my physical health hasn't been up to par. I don't feel disappointed or guilty that I didn't accomplish my goal. It was a good challenge—made me aware that it still was a good goal. I do intend to keep at it. I believe it's made me more tuned into painting, in general; and I'm improving in technique. I feel more pleased with what I've done and do have more definite plans for the future—all due to working toward my goal."

That's the right attitude! She noted the reason for her inability to reach her goal (poor health). Then she observed several positive outcomes that came from her attempting to reach her goal. That's the way to self esteem!

Goal-Setting "Work Outs"

1. Are you setting up a goal?
    (a) If so, does it check out with each of the 7 steps?
        1. Short term or mini goals to a long term goal?
        2. Is it **your** goal?
        3. Is it challenging but achievable?
        4. Is it measurable?
        5. Have you written it down and/or told a trusted friend?
        6. Is it under your control—as much as possible?
        7. Is it just *one* goal?

2. Can you remember when you failed to reach your goal?
    (a) Which item or items (1-7) caused you the trouble?
    (b) Or was it a goal that you decided not to pursue?
        1. Hopefully, you didn't flog yourself for this. It's **your** choice—to pursue it or *not.*

3. Think about a recent goal you reached.
    (a) How did it make you feel?
    (b) Allow yourself time to appreciate your success.
    (c) Be thinking of a new goal to reach for.

4. Make a note that a month from now you'll review the progress you've made over the month with setting and/or achieving your goals.
    (At the end of the month...)
    (a) Did you stick to the 7 steps?
    (b) Are you finding it easier and more satisfying to reach your goals?

5. Now that you have learned the ways to have high self esteem, go back and review the chapters which you feel you need more work on.
    (a) Make it a point to practice the skills suggested in those chapters.
    (b) Remember to be patient with yourself and **persistent!**

HOW DO YOU KEEP IT?

How To Get It Back

Now that you are familiar with the steps to gain self esteem, (**all** of which are under **your** control), I'm sure you have experienced the wonderful feeling of liking yourself most of the time. I say "most of the time," because high self esteem is *not* something that is with you all of the time. Even after learning all the skills to get it, there are "down days." Don't be discouraged when this happens; it's normal.

Self esteem fluctuates and even seems to vanish at certain moments in our lives. When we experience these periods of lack of self esteem we feel inferior, guilty, insecure, or unloved. Little things may throw us into this slump. We make a social blunder, or dress inappropriately for an occasion, or say the wrong thing. Our self esteem melts, and we are uncomfortable and anxious. We miss the feeling that we had—one of self confidence, of being lovable and competent. How do we get it back?

Once you have learned how to get this wondrous feeling of a positive self image, it's not much of a problem to get it back! The trick is to put the following "cures" into action; try not to be immobilized for long.

There are times when even the **most** self-assured individuals lose their composure, their spirit, their optimistic outlook.

Usually it is when they are tired or not feeling well. Haven't you had that experience? Just one good night's sleep has brought self esteem back as if by magic. *Awareness* is the key factor here. Be aware that self esteem is dwindling and be aware of what brings it back.

Everyone has their unique ways of recapturing self esteem— methods they have used for years without giving a thought as to why and how. Some people go for a long drive—alone—out in the country. They come back feeling "more like themselves." Some people scrub everything in sight and feel better after a period of cleaning. Some read; some go fishing, etc. These have all proved to be helpful to them for regaining their self esteem. Below is a list of these activities provided me by my workshop participants:

bake bread	listen to music
take a long walk	watch T.V.
commune with nature	do a crossword puzzle
pray	read a good book
write letters to friends	feed the birds
sew	talk about my feelings
love my pet	write down my thoughts
do something for someone	clean house
check my physical well being	go to church
have company	eat popcorn or ice cream
assert myself	go to the park
self hypnosis	ride my bike
make a list and check things off	take pictures
rationalize	take a nap
take a warm bath	cry
buy myself a present	visit older friends
show compassion	set up something to look
weigh the importance of the incident	forward to

Did you recognize some of your "sure cures" among those listed? Or there might be some there which you'll try—next time you're feeling low. Many of them could be related to your value system. This brings us to my first method of bolstering a faltering self esteem:

(1) **Act on your value system.** In Chapter 6, "Your Value System," we discussed how vital it is to your self esteem to be familiar with your value system. It is paramount to your feeling good about yourself. You can use that same value system to retrieve self esteem that has strayed. Take a look at the list of things you value about yourself and put one or two of them into **action.**

For instance, I value the fact that I'm "thoughtful" and also that "I'm a good cook." So, when I'm feeling not-so-good-about-me, I invite someone who's alone—or needs cheering up—to have dinner in my home. Just making the preparations for the meal makes me happier. By the end of the evening, I've repossessed the positive feelings about myself. It's as easy as that!

If you value the fact that you are intelligent, read a challenging article or book and reinforce the fact that you're a "super brain."

If you value your athletic ability, get out and exhibit that skill.

If you value your strength of being a friend, write a letter to a friend who is far away. Or do a favor for a friend who is close by.

Take a look at your value system and put it into action, and your self esteem will come flooding back. In all probability, it was deviating from your value system that left you without self esteem. So use your value system to put it back in working order. This all relates back to the *positive* self esteem cycle (Diagram One). When you act on your value system, you are **behaving** in a manner which brings positive reactions, which brings *thoughts* of affirmation about your worth, which brings the *feeling* of self esteem.

(2) The second method is to **realize that high self esteem is gone temporarily; it will return.**

This is something we learn from experience. When a child's world is upset, he or she feels that, "It's the end of the world. Life is cruel. I'm no good, and I never will be."

As adults, we know that we can be in deep despair—close to suicide—and, in a day or two, we feel great!

So, when you feel "in the pits," tell yourself, "This is only temporary. I can get through today, because I know tomorrow will be better. I know how to handle this."

Make sure you say words to this effect several times during that "down" period. It will rescue you from thinking that you're always going to feel that despondent.

(3) The next method is to **check out your attitude. There are three key questions to consider when using this method.**

Are you concentrating on your strengths? Do it. Other people are not always around to give you the strokes you need. Try "self-stroking"; it's a good skill to learn. When you do that, you are recognizing your strengths and focusing on your good qualities rather than your weaknesses. Or maybe you are feeling unappreciated because you haven't been getting the approval which you feel you deserve. Remember, people are often too caught up with their own problems to take the time to notice how well you did this-or-that. It's not because you didn't do it well. Sometimes, a nudge from you will cause them to take a moment to say the things they really are feeling about you. By a nudge, I mean: "What do you think of this outfit I'm wearing?" or "Wasn't that the longest ball I've hit this round?" or "Hasn't my performance improved?" This will often awaken them to the fact that they had *meant* to say something complimentary to you about these subjects, but they were just too preoccupied. They will welcome the opportunity.

Then, it often is the case that other individuals feel that you **know** you're handsome, or an expert at bridge, or dress well, or are honest, etc. — so why should they tell you what they're feeling about your superior qualities? They take it for granted that you hear it all the time; that it must be boring. So, they refrain from saying the glowing adjectives they're feeling about you for fear it will be tiresome to you. Many times people who are outstanding don't get the raves that they should for this very reason. This may be the case when you're having those feelings of not being appreciated.

But the bottom line is that **you** appreciate your strengths. Take out your strength list and luxuriate in it. Praise yourself. Realize how you've grown by putting your strengths to use!

Second key question: **Are you feeding your mind negatives?** Are you exaggerating your mistakes and trying to mind-read other people's thoughts?

Are you calling yourself names like: "Jerk," "Dope," "Stupid," "Dummy"? The *only* time that name-calling serves any productive purpose may be when you have high self esteem. The temporary tirade directed at yourself simply is saying, "You Dunce — you can do better than that — now prove it!" or "Silly, that's not your style, get with it — shape up!" If you have a good self image at the time, these comments may stimulate you to do better.

But, if you criticize yourself with negative mind-feeding when you are lacking in confidence, you just drive yourself farther into the ground and reinforce your feeling of inability and helplessness. It is imperative that you **stop** negative mind-feeding **immediately** when you have a low supply of self esteem. Replace the negatives with positives and use the thought-stopping methods of extinction.

And the final question in method three: **Are you expecting perfection of yourself?** Accept the fact that all human beings, by their very nature, are imperfect and make mistakes. Stop striving to be perfect; it can't be done. It's an unreachable goal. Instead, try some of the following:

> Work at developing an **anti**-perfectionist outlook.
>
> Laugh at yourself.
>
> Jot down all the drawbacks of perfectionism.
>
> Explain to a friend why perfectionism is self-defeating.
>
> Give yourself the right to be wrong and still love yourself.

A general attitude-overhaul is in order when you are searching for your lost self esteem. Take time to think through each of the components of your attitude and **take control** of changing them.

(4) The next important method is: **Contact a friend**—someone who thinks the sun rises and sets with you. There are times when this is the best medicine for a sick self esteem.

Of course, it is not wise **always** to depend on others for our feeling of well being; but there are times when it is healthy to use this approach. If you sprain your arm, it is sensible to wear a sling for a period until it heals. So it is with an ailing self esteem; nurture it until it is strong again. Call a friend—maybe someone from your close support group. Make plans to meet them for lunch or go for a walk—whatever the activity—just so you'll be together. That way you can feel the warmth, the love, the understanding, the support from that significant other. It will revive your faith in yourself. We never outgrow our need for that affirmation from others. This little story perhaps tells it better than any other I've read.

A little child said, "Mama, let's play a game. Let's play darts. I'll throw the darts, and you say, "**Wonderful.**"

We all need that someone to say "**wonderful**." Call or see that someone when you are feeling low.

(5) Next, **set a Goal (Instant Goal Gratification)**. Achieving or accomplishing something often takes us out of the doldrums. Be sure to use caution, however, be certain that you follow the goal-setting guidelines meticulously. A misstep here could make you feel even more inadequate. Set a fairly easy goal; one that can be reached almost *immediately*; and get busy on it! Sometimes just planning the goal is a boost to your self image. Make it a goal that you can reach that hour, that day, or by the next day—for sure. You want to feel confidence returning **soon**.

(6) The last method is: **Analyze the cause of your discomfort and confront it**. Maybe the root of your lack of self esteem has to do with a problem you're having in a relationship. You've been aware that there's a problem, and you're disgusted with yourself for avoiding the issue. Or, perhaps you don't know *how* to handle the problem.

If it's procrastination that is the concern here, you can stop that. Check into how uncomfortable you're feeling and ask yourself if it's worth it. Your reluctance to move on this problem is what's causing the pain—not the problem itself. So, tackle it today—don't leave yourself hanging.

If you don't know how to approach this situation, there are people whom you can contact. There might be a friend whom you consider wise and fair who would empathize with you and give advice if you asked. Or, seek professional help—a counselor, psychologist, or psychiatrist who will be an objective listener who will help you find alternative solutions to this dilemma.

Whatever way you choose, move on it today. Nothing can be solved by your worrying and fretting. If it's a problem with a relationship, it takes interaction with the other party or parties involved to solve it. If your poor self image is caused by a problem you detect within yourself that has nothing to do with other people, follow the same general methods. Seek out a friend whom you trust to discuss it with or consult with a professional.

Protect yourself from enduring any more painful hours. This is deadly to your self esteem.

These six methods are "tried and true" with many persons who have worked on reviving their positive self image. However, if you have your own special ways to recapture self esteem, by all means keep using them. Become acutely aware of what they are and use them when needed. Test out the six methods suggested here if they are different from your own. Use them. They will prove to be helpful to you.

Become aware also of the causes of your "lapses" in feeling confident. Once you are fully attuned to the reasons for losing self esteem and the ways to get it back, you will find it a much more pleasant life for you and those around you.

It's all within your power. You have the opportunity to be the richest person in the world: one who feels self-assured and in control of your life. Most people would give anything for this treasure. It's yours for the taking. However, I have a friend who says, "There's no free lunch; you don't get something for nothing." Now that you've learned what there is to know about getting self esteem and keeping it, your job is to **practice, have patience** and **be persistent!**

How to Get it Back "Work Outs"

1. Draw a line down the center of a blank sheet of paper. On one side of the line, write down all the words that describe how you think, act and feel when you are "down" on yourself. On the other side of the line write down all the words that describe how you think, act and feel when you have high self esteem.

   (a) Jot down your present methods of getting from the "down" side of the page to the "up" side.

2. How do the methods in 1. (a) relate to your value system?

   (a) Look at your value system and write down other activities which would put your value system into action. Keep these ideas handy for a "blue-funk" day.

3. Set your wrist watch alarm (or any other alarm clock that is available) for a convenient time during the day.

   (a) When it buzzes, think of some of your strengths.

   (b) Which strengths are you using that day?

4. Make a record of the number of times you resort to negative mind-feeding during the day or night.

   (a) As you become aware of that destructive behavior, can you lessen the number of times you do it?

   (b) Have you practiced thought-stopping lately? Read again about this method of mind control.

5. Jot down an immediate goal you could work toward. Refer to it the next time you're "down."

6. List the loved ones whom you might call on when your self esteem needs bolstering.

   (a) Do something today to maintain these relationships for they are your "self-esteem-insurance."

7. Think of a problem you have been reluctant to confront.

   (a) Move on it **today**.

   (b) If you are in a quandary as to how to approach this problem, seek personal or professional help.

8. Have you made a mistake lately?

   (a) If it was a little one—forget it, it isn't worth worrying about.

   (b) If it was a big one—be glad you've made it; you'll never make it again.

Conclusion

It would be wonderful, after reading about the fundamentals for self esteem building, if you could simply review them in your mind and say, "Now I've got it!" Unfortunately, it's not that easy. It takes time and effort to build or improve anything. Self esteem is no exception. In order to have high self esteem, you must **practice,** have **patience** and be **persistent.**

First, let's consider **practice.** If you were attempting to build up your muscle tone, you would set up a series of exercises and do them on a regular basis. It would do absolutely no good to exercise frantically only at the times you were feeling weak and out of shape.

So it is with self-esteem-building. It is essential that you exercise these techniques regularly — until they become involuntary responses. It is helpful to know how to get self esteem *back*, but why lose it in the first place? If you practice the work outs several times a week, that's the best preventative program for keeping that incomparable feeling of loving youself. Practice **all** of the areas. You may need more work on your value system than you do on recognizing your strengths. So, naturally, that's where you will put the most effort. But, the entire spectrum of self-esteem-building needs attention: your attitude, value system, support system and goal setting. It takes all of these components to develop a strong self esteem—just as you must exercise your entire body to have true physical fitness.

It would be advisable for you to set aside a portion of each day for **practicing** the suggestions in the work outs. You can do them alone; or, as many people do, with a friend—or in a group. However you choose to practice—**do it!** Regrettably, practicing the activities for creating a good self image is akin to exercising your body to stay in shape. All goes well if you are consistent about practicing several times a week. If, however, you desist from this regimen, your body will return to its original flabby self; similarly, with lack of exercise, your self image will disintegrate into a feeling of insecurity and incompetence. Practice is required if you wish to keep a strong, positive self concept.

Next comes **patience.** They say that patience is a virtue; some people have it, and some don't. In the case of self-esteem-building, patience is a *necessity*. You may practice diligently and still feel that you're not making much headway. Discouragement creeps in. That's a "downer" for a positive self image. Before thoughts of giving up take over, employ patience. Realize that changing a pattern you've had for years is difficult to do. Your old habits seemed more comfortable—even the destructive ones—so you lapse back into your familiar ways that do nothing to raise your self esteem. Recognizing this, you may become irritated with your lack of discipline. Have patience; it takes time to change. Give yourself the benefit of that time.

If a "work out" doesn't change your life—overnight—be patient. These are new skills which will require many periods of practicing to become natural and part of your mode of life. Don't expect a dramatic change after a try or two. It may take many attempts and many hours, but the results will be rewarding. To approve of yourself automatically is a feeling worth all the hours of effort.

This practicing and using patience isn't always easy; there is no magic wand. It takes constant awareness and energy. That's where **persistence** comes in. If you don't get it the first time, try it again—and again. One flex of the arm doesn't make a firm and bulging muscle; it has to be flexed over and over. You can't lose five pounds by pushing away from the table once or twice; it takes persistence. So be persistent. Repeat the "work outs" until they become second-nature to you.

The more you exercise the skills for acquiring self esteem, the easier and more productive they will become. You'll find yourself thinking of them more and more during your daily activities. Before long, you will react spontaneously, both in thoughts and actions, to the principles which create the feeling of high self esteem. That's the pay-off for all your practice, patience and persistence.

In this age, humans travel faster and farther, have robots to do their work, have found cures for diseases, can successfully implant organs, **but** each of us is left with the task and opportunity of being in charge of our self esteem. As I explained at the beginning of the book—you are the "self" in this self help book. It takes you to carry out the suggestions in order to make the changes you desire. Nobody can do it for you, but you **can** do it.

You can do it, because you are in control of the four basics for having high self esteem:

1. Your attitude, which includes recognizing your strengths, not trying to be perfect, and eliminating the negative mind-feeding.

2. Living by your value system.

3. Checking your support system.

4. Setting goals—following the seven steps.

These basics are producers of self esteem; and they're all within your power to manage and regulate. With them you will learn to appreciate and like yourself. It is uncomfortable and irksome to go through life with someone you don't like. Wherever you go, whatever you do, **you** are there. You have the capability of making your life more pleasant.

This is not to say that there won't be times when your solid self esteem weakens; that's normal. Nobody rides the crest of high self esteem every minute. But, generally, it will be higher and more constant than before. After all, you now know how to develop an optimum self concept and get it back when it seems to elude you. So, by using the three P's—practice, patience and persistence—the payoff will be to feel more loving of yourself most of the time; you will have fewer "low" periods, and they will be of shorter duration and less traumatic. That will free you to live a full-functioning, useful, meaningful, productive life—one that will give you feelings of satisfaction and pride. This will bring peace and happiness into your life which you can get no other way.

"Love of others and love of ourselves are not alternatives. On the contrary, an attitude of love towards themselves will be found in all those who are capable of loving others."

Eric Fromm

Action Plan

The final "work out" that is necessary after practicing all the others is to develop your **action plan** for acquiring self esteem. In setting up your action plan, follow the seven steps of goal setting. The first two steps, as you remember, are to identify a short term goal and be sure that it is something **you** want to do.

The format for your action plan should be as follows:

What Am I Willing to Do?

Confront a destructive person in my support system.

When?

This week.

My Supports		**My Roadblocks**	
(Internal)	**(External)**	**(Internal)**	**(External)**
Determination. Understanding that it is good for both of us. Courage. Convinced that it's vital to my having a healthy self image.	My close support group.	Not wanting to hurt this person. Fear of ending the relationship.	The destructive person's temper.

The example incorporates the other steps for goal setting: be sure that the goal is attainable, measurable, written down, under your control (as much as possible), and just one goal at a time.

If this were your action plan, the internal and external supports are important for you to be aware of in case you need help along the way with this plan; it may be a difficult one for you. However, you must have thought it was achievable or you wouldn't have chosen it as your goal. Right?

The purpose of considering the roadblocks—both internal and external—is to prepare you for what could happen to interfere with your "hoped for" consequences of the action plan. The goal is under your control; you can confront this destructive person. The outcome, however, cannot be assured since another person is involved besides yourself. In realizing this, you won't be disappointed in yourself or angry if the confrontation doesn't bring the results you are hoping for. You will feel good about yourself for carrying out your action plan of talking with the destructive person in your support system.

The person whom you are confronting will either decide that the friendship is worth keeping—and change his or her behavior; or, decide not to. That is a risk that you were aware of when you conceived the plan. It was clearly stated in the internal supports that you were convinced that this was the proper action to take—regardless of the consequences. You obviously felt that it was worth it to your self esteem to live without this destructive friend. Either a change would be made, or the relationship would have to go.

The example may not be one that suits your needs. Choose an action plan which fits for you; one that's achievable and is in an area for building self esteem where you need more work.

These examples of action plans may help you in formulating yours:

> Learn to know my strengths
> Stop negative mind-feeding
> Stop trying to be perfect
> Get my value system in order and live by it
> Take better care of my health
> Set a positive goal

Do more for my close support group
Get in touch with a prospective friend
Practice thought-stopping when I'm negative
Stop overeating
Graduate from college next semester

When you have designated the subject of your plan, place it into the "Action Plan Format" and complete the appropriate details under each of the headings. Then, put your plan into action!

Once you have completed that action plan for self esteem, take time to appreciate your accomplishment and then—start another one! These will be your "**original** work outs" which you can fashion to fit any problems you may be having at that moment with your self image. They will be your personal exercises to enhance and strengthen your self esteem.

The result of all your time and energy spent will be your ability to live from inside out, rather than from outside in. You will feel capable, adequate, competent, lovable and sure on the *inside*. Therefore, your actions, on the *outside*, will be productive, caring, energetic, happy, and self-actualizing. Nothing forced and nothing phony—just beautiful **you**—giving to the world all that is in you to give. You are free to be yourself. And you will know that you are loved, truly loved, just for being **you**.

Go for it! How do you love **you**? Start counting the ways . . .